The Oz Syndrome

Finding Contentment in Your Family

Michael O'Donnell

HillCrest
PUBLISHING

The Oz Syndrome: Finding Contentment in Your Family

1648 Campus Court
Abilene, TX 79601
Typesetting by Fritz Miller Studio
Copyright © 2001
Michael O'Donnell

Printed in the United States of America

ISBN 0-89112-480-2

Library of Congress Card Number 2001088095

To my twin brother, Richard Allen O'Donnell—who can impersonate every character in *The Wizard of Oz*—your love and loyalty were my first clues that "There's no place like home!"

Acknowledgements

Special thanks must go to Michael Blanton, a dear brother whose encouragement places him second only to Barnabas and without whom this book might never have been published.

Thanks also to Wes Yoder, who looked out for my best interests—my family is especially appreciative.

Thanks to Joey Paul, who never stopped believing in this project—your personal encouragement and professional guidance mean so much to me. And to Lyn Wheeler, Pamela McClure, and Byron Williamson—thank you for your kind support.

To my publisher, Thom Lemmons, who has brought freshness and friendship to this project, I say thank you for both.

To my friend Sue Hoon, who is a word processor "par excellence," I say thank you for preserving my sanity.

And to my family—especially Becky and Bruce, Richard, David and Sandra—I love you. To my mom and dad, *thank you*. And to my precious wife, Rachel, and equally precious children—Patrick, Cara, and Kayla—you make coming home so easy!

Contents

Introduction

Born with just 40 percent of her brain, Cara lived only two months but gave my family a lifetime of joy. Without uttering a single word—not even a coo or a gurgle—Cara taught us to value family life and a God who works in the most difficult and seemingly senseless circumstances. Her gifts to us were a lesson in unconditional love and a renewed faith in God that makes our final journey home—and heavenly reward— eagerly anticipated. What I am about to share will not be easy for me. My life has been touched and forever changed by a severely handicapped baby who never walked, talked, or laughed but who taught me and my family much about life— even in death.

This is the story of Cara Marie O'Donnell and her family. As her father, I intend to tell the story from my point of view and share with you some of the things I felt and saw during the two months Cara was with us on earth. Later I will present the story from my wife's point of view, told as only a mother could put it into words.

We first learned that my wife, Rachel, was pregnant with our second child at the end of September 1990. Our new baby was due to be born July 6 of the following year. Rachel's parents flew to Texas just a few hours before the delivery to be with their daughter. Everything seemed perfect. I had gone to the office to catch up on some work while Rachel and her mother went to the grocery store to get food for our evening meal. At the store, Rachel went into labor. This both surprised and delighted us, as very few women actually deliver on their due date.

We called the doctor. Our primary care physician was not available, so we waited for the doctor on call to phone us back. The phone call came with instructions, "Go to the hospital and wait for me there."

By the time we reached the hospital, Rachel had dilated to eight centimeters. The baby was coming faster than the doctor on call could respond. One of the nurses in the delivery room found an ob-gyn to deliver our child.

I watched as a beautiful little girl entered our world. All I could think was, "How wonderful!" God had answered my prayers for a daughter! Our family would now be complete.

But something was wrong. I could tell! Cara appeared weak and unstable. Her hand and body motions were visibly peculiar, and there seemed to be a tiny tick or some type of seizure activity about her right eye and near the corner of her mouth. Teaching infant development at a nearby university didn't make matters any better for me, as I began to clinically ponder the abnormal appearance of our child.

I immediately began to ask questions. Nobody dared volunteer an answer. There was a strange denial going on as the doctor who delivered Cara cleaned up and left as quickly as he came. The nurses moved about the delivery room in silence. No congratulations... no words of cheer... just concerned and anxious looks as our baby was whisked away.

Without my saying anything, my wife knew—right off the bat—that something had gone terribly wrong. Still, neither of us said aloud what we both suspected. We kept our opinions and our secret fears to ourselves.

I left Rachel in the delivery room to recover and followed the nurses to the hospital's neonatal ward. Cara was put under a sun lamp. She was having trouble regulating her temperature and her breathing now appeared irregular. I was numb. I couldn't believe this was happening... not to our little girl... not to this sweet, tender child—the result of prayer after prayer for divine safety during all nine months of her prenatal development.

Almost instinctively I began to check her fingers and toes. No Down's syndrome. What, then? Fear began to grip me as I contemplated the alternatives. Seizure activity. "Please, God, no! Not something wrong with her brain!" I

3

began to pray that I had been wrong and that it was Down's, after all. I had been particularly fond of a little girl with that disease earlier in my teaching career. Maybe God was preparing me for Cara with that previous experience. "I can handle that," I thought. "Please, God, let it be Down's.... Anything but the alternatives .... Please, God, please!" My silent, inward pleading continued as I held my baby's face in my hands.

Rachel was finally brought up in a wheelchair and placed in the room where I had been standing watch over Cara.

"What's wrong with our baby?" asked Rachel.

"You tell me, Rachel. Tell me what you think it is."

"Down's syndrome?"

"I don't think so."

"Then what, Michael?"

"I don't know." We grabbed each other's hands and began to weep very quietly to ourselves. It seemed an eternity before we were finally given some answers.

The answers were not good. Apparently, our precious newborn had a severe brain anomaly known as holoprosencephaly. We were told she was going to die. We could not believe our ears. It was as though we were like some electric appliance whose plug had been pulled. We just stood there motionless, frozen with shock, suspended in time. Neither of us could move. We could barely speak. We just stared at Cara for the longest time. Slowly my wife's anguish began to fill the air—little, almost inaudible cries at first, then uncontrollable sobbing followed by hot, gushing tears. I joined her in our grief and also began to cry aloud. The pain was immense. But it was just the beginning.

No one could have prepared us for what was to come. The prospect of a loved one's death—and particularly that of a child—has a way of clarifying what is really important in this world. Like nothing else, an infant doomed to die pulls us back from the urgent to the truly important things in life. We gain perspective as we move through stages of shock and disbelief to the ever-recurring question of our own finiteness. We perhaps begin to question (as I did) what we want to do next with the few remaining years we have left this side of heaven.

As someone has wisely discerned: "I don't know of any executive while on his death bed who wished he had spent more time at work."

What was I spending most of my time doing? Working, of course!

Cara's birth changed all that. The long hours at work or on the road stopped. Family concerns became my life. Holding Cara. Feeding Cara. Changing Cara. Bathing Cara. Needing Cara to stay alive... comforting my wife and son because we knew she wouldn't .... These issues became central to me.

My speaking engagements now included the entire family. Nestled away in some nearby hotel would be Rachel, Patrick, and Cara. I would go to speak, then quickly disappear afterwards to rush back to the hotel and spend all the time I could with them. There were times when Rachel and I didn't sleep all night because we were up comforting Cara, but somehow God would empower me to speak before thousands the following day, filling me with words clearly beyond my own abilities. There were the cancellations, too, and the angry, disappointed responses from conference planners who couldn't or wouldn't understand why my family had to come first.

It was during this time that I began to refocus on my marriage as well.

Rachel became more than a wife to me, she became my best friend. As I watched her handle and gently, lovingly care for our only daughter, my appreciation for her grew. She was marvelous! She was beyond what I could ever have hoped or imagined for a wife and a mother for our children. She taught me much, simply by my observing her.

There were times when I would sneak out of bed and find her early in the morning, tending to Cara's needs. (There were many complicated and laborious medical procedures to contend with.) Rachel would gently rock her to sleep, holding her for hours on end in a position that was comfortable to Cara but painfully awkward for her. She would dress her in the most beautiful of early childhood outfits, with precious "head pretties" and bows.

When seeing Cara for the first time, many would even wonder: "What's wrong with her?" Because of the care of a loving mother, Cara's physical anomalies were barely visible now. Rachel made sure of that. Cara would be treated like any other newborn—with all the grace and dignity such precious little ones deserve. Seemingly endless, sleepless hours with many visits to the doctor's office, and eventually an air ambulance ride to a children's hospital in Fort Worth became our way of life. When Cara was hospitalized, we all camped out in her room—Rachel, Patrick, and me. We would rarely leave her side. Whispered prayers and Bible readings became our daily bread.

The Bible passages about a mother letting go and saying good-bye, for instance, were extremely moving. From the story of Hannah, who gave her just-weaned son, Samuel, to be raised by Eli the priest of the Hebrew temple at Shiloh (see 1 Sam. 1:21–28) to the story of Rachel who, as a metaphor, wept for the slaughtered children of Bethlehem and refused to be comforted "because they are no more" (Matt, 2:16–18), Rachel learned from Bible examples that a mother's final good-bye is a painful one.

It was equally true for my wife.

I share excerpts from her own journal because they express so well what we both experienced—but only Rachel could have put into words the bittersweet joy of knowing Cara and the pain of losing her:

August 4, 1991

I have been constantly amazed at how people have given of

themselves to make us feel loved. We have been given lots of flowers .... The flower arrangement that really touched me was the one sent by Harold and Jeanette. They sent a single pink rose bud inside a potted plant. When it first came I stared at it all day long. The rose bud made me think of Cara. It looked so vulnerable and soft and it was still closed up—just like Cara is a blossom not yet opened. The next day the rose bud had wilted and died before it opened, but the plant remains and grows on.

I felt like I had watched our lives portrayed in flowers and plants. Cara will not be opened until she is in heaven with God.

Some people pray for a miracle that God will cause Cara's brain to be whole. I believe God can do that, but I don't think He will. I believe Cara has come into the world so God's power and glory will be manifested in those around Cara.

It would be easy for God to heal my baby, but instead I hear Him saying, "Trust and believe in Me. Cara is already pure and fit for the Kingdom. She will never be touched by the evil one. It is for you that I send this tender package of vulnerable innocence. I send her so you will not fear death; to make the Kingdom real; and to show you the love I have for you.

"See how your daughter brings people to My throne—some asking why this has happened? Some begging for strength. And some praying for a miracle. Cara, just by being, has brought focus to Me .... Sweet daughter, do not fear; just believe. There is purpose and I have chosen you to bear the burden of this purpose.

"I know of your burden and of the injustice you feel. I sent My son to be born and to die. I know what it is like to lose a child and I weep for your pain.

"Cling to Me and I will sustain you and will not allow your spirit to be quenched. My strength will make you strong. I will send the Holy Spirit to you in many ways. Sometimes it will be through people of the Kingdom. Sometimes He will come when you are alone and your heart is heavy. And sometimes He will come as a word from Me. Trust and believe."

August 29, 1991

I got up around 7 a.m.. I needed to feed Cara, get dressed, and get Patrick ready for Rainbow Bible School. I finished feeding Cara around 8:30 that morning. I set her up in her bassinet so that her food would stay down more easily. I told Michael that she needed to stay upright for awhile until her food started to digest.

I was feeling rather frantic because I didn't want to be late on Patrick's second day of school. Patrick and I were finally ready to go and I went in to say good-bye to Michael. I wanted Patrick to hurry, but he kept trying to kiss Cara good-bye. I finally let Patrick get near to where he could kiss Cara and then we were off to school.

When I finally got home it was 9:50 and Michael told me Cara had been having "blue spells" and he had been afraid to leave her alone.

I picked her up out of her bassinet and changed her position, hoping it would help her breathe. I watched her for a few minutes and saw she was still blue. I picked her up again. That's when she stopped breathing for the first time.

I called to Michael and he said to lay her down on our bed. He called his office and told them Cara was having some problems breathing and that he wasn't coming in. We knew she was going to die very soon.

We kept telling Cara she had our permission to go and to look for the children, because now she was to play with them. We also told her to take Jesus' hand—that He was there to love her. We told her to go to the light, because in the light was Jesus and in that light she would be whole and warm and happy.

We thought it would be easy to let her go and in one sense it was. But in another sense, we wanted desperately to keep her with us.... I believe my voice comforted her.... When she finally stopped breathing we just sat with her in silence. Michael put his ear to Cara's chest and said her heart had stopped. She was gone. We just cried and cried. I picked Cara up and rocked with her. I gave her to Michael and he rocked with her.

After a bit, I took Cara while Michael called our family doctor. I went into Patrick's room to pick out a dress, shoes, and "head pretty" for Cara to wear. I took her into the bathroom. I could hardly see through my tears as I gently poured water over Cara's body.

I said to her over and over again—she was okay now. She was finally at home with Jesus.

I sat down with Patrick on his bed that evening and told him Cara was gone and that she was with Jesus Patrick, just two years old, repeated what I had said and then in a prayer spoke these words: "Good-bye, baby Cara."

No one could have prepared me for the deep valley I would fall into after Cara died. Holding her in my arms and rocking her lifeless body back and forth was more than I could bear. I threw my head back and began to plead with God to revive her. Saying farewell to an infant seemed somehow more tragic than saying good-bye to an aging parent or grandparent at a nearby nursing home. So much life unlived. So much human potential unrealized. Cara had her whole life ahead of her, but was only able to live a small fraction of it. Her short life and subsequent death proved to be a wake-up call for me.

I began to contemplate the temporary nature of life here on earth when compared to eternity with God. I thought about a daughter who would now be living in a totally Christ-centered environment. Angels would be her constant companions. Cherubim and seraphim would be her guides. Her concerns would be spiritual rather than physical.

It even began to dawn on me that soon I would be joining her world—a spiritual world vastly different from the one she left behind. To relate to a daughter literally raised in the presence of God meant that my priorities would have to change. Her treasures would be different from the things I had come to embrace in this temporal world of the living.

"What will we talk about?" I pondered.

I wondered: "Will we have anything in common?" She would no doubt marvel that I had placed so much importance on things. She wouldn't grasp the significance of any human accomplishment, apart from my bringing others to Christ or exhibiting his fruit in my life. Academic degrees... awards... even writing books would be insignificant in her world where worshiping God in spirit and in truth is the ultimate achievement for those now saved by grace.

Oh, Cara will teach me much!

Her spiritual sensibilities will render mine ordinary or

even obsolete by comparison. What I have faith in she will know as fact. What I hope for, she will have already achieved.

But love will be the common denominator! What she loves can be what I love, if I make a conscious decision to put people ahead of things. Her treasures can become my treasures. Her experiences mine, if I put on love—God's love... love that knows no bounds. "It always protects, always trusts, always hopes, always perseveres" (1 Cor. 13:7). It's what makes life here on earth meaningful and full of great purpose.

To love our families as we have been loved by God becomes our sole legitimate ambition, a source of true contentment and ultimate fulfillment for the restless heart. It is how we *live,* so we don't have to look back and say: "Oh, how I've wasted my life."

With Cara's death and the prospect of my own mortality close at hand came the desire to live life differently. I wanted fewer regrets. I wanted fulfillment and a restful heart. I wanted contentment. I wanted things that last—well into eternity! Yet I soon learned it would take more than saying good-bye to my daughter. It would also mean saying good-bye to my lifelong search for having it all! But how would I discover another way? How would I gain contentment? How would I ever find a way of living that encompassed both the present and eternity?

I believe I have discovered some answers in paralleling a modern-day parable to help address these age-old questions. It is a popular movie most everyone knows, L. Frank Baum's children's classic, *The Wizard of Oz*. This marvelous odyssey of pop culture contains several deeply-rooted clues to help us learn how to fulfill our restless hearts and find contentment through trials like those Dorothy and her friends endured on their journey to the mythical land of Oz.

PART ONE

The Oz Syndrome

"The Oz Syndrome" is a term I've coined to describe what most people go through in their search for answers to life's basic challenges. Like Dorothy and her three traveling companions—the Scarecrow, the Tin Man, and the Lion—they wind up going on a strange and difficult journey over the rainbow and down the yellow brick road, hoping to receive from a wizard what they in fact already possess. The wizard represents those forces outside oneself that seem to offer up all those easy answers.

What Dorothy learns is that the answers are not to be found in the *fabled* Emerald City.

Why? Because they were there all along.

Part One *reviews this process as it plays itself out in* The Wizard of Oz *story.* Chapter 1 *reviews the journey of Dorothy and her three traveling companions into the Land of Oz.* Chapter 2 *examines the things that the wizards of Oz—the places we go to find answers to life's problems—can and cannot give us.* Chapter 3 *takes Dorothy back home to Kansas, where she examines what she learned during her difficult adventure.*

One

Dorothy and Her Three Companions in Oz

Dorothy and her three companions—the Scarecrow, the Tin Man, and the Lion—are convinced they each lack something to be whole, happy beings. The Scarecrow needs a brain. The Tin Man lacks a heart. The Lion lacks courage. And Dorothy just wants a better life.

As we watch the four oddly matched companions travel

the yellow brick road in the MGM movie version of L. Frank Baum's classic tale, we notice that each friend exhibits the very virtues all say they lack.

When Dorothy is scolded by talking trees for picking their apples, it is the Scarecrow who puts a finger to the side of his head as if in deep thought, and says: "I'll show you how to get apples." And he does! No apparent lack of brainpower here!

Likewise, the Tin Man continually demonstrates his compassion and tender spirit. He cries at even the thought of any ill will toward Dorothy: "Oh, I just hate to think of her in the castle of the Wicked Witch! We've got to get her out." And they do, led by the heroic and courageous efforts of the so-called Cowardly Lion.

Even when they finally do meet the real Wizard of Oz and persuade him to reach into his black bag and give them what they want, all he does is acknowledge—with physical signs and symbols—what they have always possessed. The diploma for the Scarecrow, the heart-shaped pocket watch for the Tin Man, and the medal of valor for the Lion are simply outward tokens of inward realities.

Even Dorothy, who wants to escape over the rainbow to seek after her own heart's desire—the better life—winds up back home in Kansas, filled with fresh awareness that if what she seeks is not in her own backyard then she really hasn't lost anything to begin with. Finally she learns that she doesn't have to travel all the way to Oz to find contentment. She discovers that she can find contentment right at home!

Her discovery reaffirms a time-honored idea that "home is where the heart is"... that, indeed, the most fulfilling experiences are with those of our own household... and that, yes—when all is said and done—"there's no place like home!"

I realize this theme is not new and can be seen in any number of ancient proverbs, like these:

- "The grass is always greener on the other side of the fence."
- "A bird in the hand is worth two in the bush."
- "To arrive is better than to trust hopefully."

All such sayings remind us that we should be content with what we have. We should strive to make what we have even better. Scriptures, moreover, clearly teach that we ought not be anxious for tomorrow, but rather by prayer and petition, with thanksgiving, we ought to present our requests to God. "'And the peace of God," writes Paul, "which transcends all understanding, will guard your hearts and minds in Christ Jesus" (Phil. 4:7). Certainly, Paul's wise counsel to his spiritual son, Timothy, says it all: "For we brought nothing into the world, and we can take nothing out of it. But if we have food and clothing, we will be content with that" (1 Tim. 6:7-8).

Here's where the movie version of *The Wizard of* Oz beautifully fits in. Dorothy eventually learns that running away solves few problems—and sometimes creates new ones! After all, it is Dorothy's home back in Kansas that holds the answers to life's difficulties, not some magical, mythical place called Oz.

I believe that's what draws us to the film in the first place. Almost sixty years ago—and over a billion viewers later—MGM's *The Wizard of Oz* remains one of the most beloved films ever made. In the words of the Academy Award-winning actress, Angela Lansbury, "[*The Wizard of Oz* is] a movie filled with values that we all cherish .... A movie for all of us; for all time."

Thus, I want to share with you these "cherished" values as we tour the mythical land of Oz together so that we might learn—as did Dorothy—that life's most sought-after treasures are closer than we think.

SOMEWHERE OVER THE RAINBOW:
THE SEARCH FOR CONTENTMENT

The Wizard of Oz begins with Dorothy running home, distraught after an apparent mishap with the forbidding Miss Gulch. She stops only long enough to make sure her dog, Toto, is all right. "Did she hurt you?" she asks, half expecting Toto to answer. "She tried to, didn't she?" After examining Toto, Dorothy quickly continues her trek toward home. "Come on, we'll go tell Uncle Henry and Auntie Em." Justice, Dorothy thinks, is just a few steps away.

How familiar this sounds! The way we handle family difficulties often leaves little to be desired. To illustrate the point, let's listen to the following conversation between an eight-year-old boy and his mother, one day after school.

We begin with Junior running through the front door with tears in his eyes, shouting, "He hit me! He hit me!"

"Who hit you, darling?" asks his mother.

"My teacher, Mr. Fenderton, that's who!" Junior is in the third grade.

"Well, Son," she inquires, "what did you do to anger Mr. Fenderton?"

Hardly the response Junior is seeking. "I didn't do anything," he sobs. Junior is now defensive.

"Well, you must have done something," insists his mother. "Now what was it?"

Sensing no sympathy here, Junior runs back out the front door feeling both unappreciated and misunderstood. Certainly, that was not what mother was attempting to do.

The breakdown here is in the way both mother and son communicate. Unfortunately feelings are often ignored or even judged until we get what we believe are the much-needed facts. Right? Ours is an attempt to approach the emotional with the logical. But people are not always rational, are they? Certainly not eight-year-old boys.

Remember, Junior had come home with real feelings of hurt, regardless of whether or not he had done anything to deserve them. His search, then, was only for comfort and a listening ear. Finding neither, he simply ran away. Sound familiar?

Let's go back to Dorothy. Once in the safe presence of family, she blurts out, "Auntie Em, just listen to what Miss

Gulch did to Toto."

"Dorothy, Dorothy... we're busy!' is the disappointing reply. Relentless in her desire to be heard, Dorothy now turns to her three friends, Hunk, Zeke, and Hickory (who become in Oz the Scarecrow, the Tin Man, and the Lion). Unfortunately, their approach is just too logical. Like contemporary counterparts to the friends of Job, they begin to offer Dorothy "constructive" criticism.

"Why, you'd think you didn't have any brains," says Hunk.

"I have too got brains," insists Dorothy.

"Then why don't you use them?" Hunk retorts.

Unfortunately, Hickory's advice is no better. "Show a little backbone... a little courage .... Just go right up to Miss Gulch and spit in her eye." Exasperated, Dorothy responds: "Oh... you just won't listen, that's all."

Adding her final thoughts on the matter, Auntie Em dismisses Dorothy's feelings with the words: "Stop imagining things... You always work yourself up into a fret over nothing... You just help us out today and find a place where you won't get into any trouble."

What follows next is really quite appropriate, when you think about it. Nothing could have been more revealing of Dorothy's frustration and her desire for escape than Harburg's and Arlen's Academy Award-winning song, "Somewhere Over the Rainbow."

When listening to that song it's no wonder that we also find ourselves caught up in Dorothy's talk about a land she has heard of once in a lullaby. We can picture Dorothy as a little girl nestled securely in her mother's arms—being lulled to sleep with thoughts of a place "where troubles melt like lemon drops away above the chimney tops" and "clouds are far behind me."

The song's tender conclusion is a subtle reminder to us of all of life's bitter limitations. "Birds fly over the rainbow," laments Dorothy. "Why then, oh why, can't I?"

Thus, the stage is set for Dorothy's greatest disappointment of all. Her furry companion—silent, but always near—is taken from her. Not only separated from Toto, but fearing his death, Dorothy is now found sprawled across her bed in absolute despair.

But moments later, Toto escapes. Reunited, the dog and girl are next seen wandering away from home—a sight all too common in America today.

Dorothy and Toto soon encounter Professor Marvel (who becomes the Wizard). He asks, "Who might you be? Don't tell me....You're running away."

"That's right," says Dorothy.

"Now why are you running away? No, no don't tell me," insists Professor Marvel. "They don't understand you at home.... They don't appreciate you.... You want to see other lands—big cities, big mountains, big oceans."

"Why, it's just like you can read what's inside of me," Dorothy exclaims.

Of course, he really can't. But that's not the point. It's

that someone has finally heard her and acknowledged her thoughts and feelings—someone, unfortunately, other than her family.

A similar thing happened to Gary. He recalls the time he had waited all day to see his friend, Bob. But Bob's attention was divided that evening between Gary and Bob's six-year-old son, Robby. Frustrated by Robby's continual interruptions with questions regarding this or that, Gary asks Bob why he permits this peculiar behavior.

"Well," explains Bob, "it's my belief that I'm creating an environment in which Robby can always know that his questions are welcomed. You see, Gary, if my son were to believe that I didn't have time or simply wasn't interested in answering his questions, then he might well seek answers from someone else. And I wouldn't be sure," Bob concluded, "what those answers might be."

Fortunately Professor Marvel is both clever and kind and creates the notion that Dorothy may well be breaking her Auntie Em's heart. He convinces her to return home.

But it's too late. Dorothy and Toto run smack-dab into a tornado of monstrous proportions. Her Auntie Em begins to desperately call aloud, "Dorothy! Dorothy!" But the roaring noise of the twister drowns her out. Forced into the storm cellar by high winds and roaring thunder, Auntie Em, Uncle Henry, and the farm hands Hunk, Zeke, and Hickory close the cellar doors on Dorothy's only refuge from the vicious storm.

In absolute fear, Dorothy runs into the house, chased by the force of the tornado that has already ripped the front door off its hinges. With no one to be found, the structure that just moments earlier housed both family and friends proves a poor haven in Dorothy's frantic search for safety. Suddenly a window explodes inward and Dorothy is struck a near-fatal blow.

Now unconscious, Dorothy begins to slip from her world... into a faraway place called Munchkin County in the mythical land of Oz.

Bill tells a similar story from real life about how his family was torn apart by a horrible disaster. "My mother and father died in a plane crash," he recalls. "I was sent to live with my aunt and uncle.

"Unfortunately we didn't get along. At least, that's how I felt at the time. I got the idea that a foster home might be a welcome alternative. It was a kind of fantasy for me that somehow life could be easier and less complicated if I were taken from my aunt and uncle and placed among total strangers. You guessed it! I was miserable, and all I kept telling everyone is that I wanted to go home. Nothing, I finally learned, can ever take the place of your own flesh and blood."

Dorothy is about to learn the same thing.

Opening the back door to her house, Dorothy and Toto step out into a Munchkin wonderland—with crystal blue lakes, beautiful flowers of every shape and kind, and smart little homes and shops. It is a far cry from the drab midwestern towns and vast farm-lands that compose her own backyard. Dorothy whispers to Toto, "I don't think we're in Kansas anymore!"

Dorothy is instantly hailed as a good witch by the Munchkins, who believe she has fallen from a star to deliver them from the oppressive powers of the Wicked Witch of the East. How did she do it? By "neatly and so completely" dropping a house on her!

Almost immediately, however, Dorothy begins to ask about a way to get back to Kansas. She soon discovers that being over the rainbow isn't all it's cracked up to be. This becomes even more evident when she learns to her absolute horror that another witch exists—the Wicked Witch of the West. "And, she's worse than the other one," warns Glenda, the Good Witch of the North, who has peacefully appeared to her among the Munchkins.

Now more anxious than ever to find a way back home, Dorothy listens as Glenda suggests that she get some help from the Wizard of Oz. But because she is without a broom-stick, Glenda recommends that Dorothy walk the winding yellow brick road which leads to the Emerald City.

Dorothy heeds her advice and without a moment's hesitation is off to see the Wizard—the wonderful Wizard of Oz. Dorothy has not yet found the contentment she seeks so she moves on restlessly, seeking answers ever further from home.

FOLLOWING THE YELLOW BRICK ROAD

Following the yellow brick road becomes a journey of hope for Dorothy. With the humorous prompting of Munchkins, like little voices speaking to the subconscious mind, we hear the words: "Follow the yellow brick road... follow, follow, follow, follow... follow the yellow brick road."

Many of us can probably remember as a child sitting absolutely spellbound in front of the TV, watching Dorothy and her friends journey that yellow brick road. No matter how many times we saw the film, each time seemed like the first time. Like the Oz characters themselves, we too walked the yellow brick road, caught up in great expectations of what would greet us at the other end.

Dorothy's journey of hope becomes our journey of hope. Haven't we all at times imagined a land "somewhere over the rainbow" that might well hold the answers? Remember longing for a land "behind the moon; beyond the rain" that could provide escape from this life and all of its unfairness?

It may be that the Scarecrow's journey of hope is our journey of hope, or perhaps the Tin Man's or the Lion's. Like Dorothy and her friends, we follow the yellow brick road looking for what we imagine to be absent from our lives. Whether it is the search for knowledge, compassion, strength, or simply our own heart's desire, we identify with the Oz characters because we feel a void that cannot be filled. "If I only had so-and-so" becomes our quest and our ultimate search for contentment. So we continue to travel the yellow brick road....

But what begins as a pleasant journey from Munchkin Land soon turns into a frightening encounter with the Wicked Witch and her evil magic. Even fantasy has its drawbacks. Here we encounter the world of the Wicked Witch of the West. Unlike the beautiful fantasyland of the Munchkins, this scary land has lions, and tigers, and bears. ("Oh, my!") In this wicked place we encounter predators of the flesh, where "might is right" and the weak are routinely preyed upon by the strong.

The terrain of the Haunted Forest of the Wicked Witch of the West seems strangely familiar to us. It is the world we experience every day. We need only pick up a local newspaper to read about it and its daily horrors of rape, teenage suicide, elder abuse, domestic violence, and crimes of passion and profit. We recognize this "wasteland" as the breeding ground of despair where loneliness hangs in the air like thick smoke after a battle—choking the life out of all who did not heed the warning: "I'd Turn Back If I Were You!"

By contrast, there soon appears the "great and powerful" Wizard. He lives in a fantastic place known as the Emerald City because of its jewel-like appearance. It is here that we find refuge and escape—comforted, for a time, in the merry old land of Oz.

Two

The Wizard of Oz

We really believe the Wizard can help us! He is, after all, the reason we've come such a long way. Following the yellow brick road we even announce our intentions while singing: "We're off to see the Wizard, the wonderful Wizard of Oz ....We hear he is a whiz of a wiz, if ever a whiz there was ....The wonderful Wizard of Oz." We believe what we've been told, that—however mysterious—the Wizard is very, very powerful. Such power, we reason, will most certainly enable the Wizard to give us what we need. Some things the Wizard can give us, but other things he can't.

WHAT THE WIZARD OF OZ CAN GIVE US

Ours is an uncanny hope—unexplainable in human terms—whereby we seek from without what we perceive to be missing from within. It stems from the inadequacy we all feel—that feeling of being somehow less than normal. "It's because I'm presumin'," says the Scarecrow, "that I could be kind of human, if I only had a brain."

Many of us have often felt the same way. Mary, for instance, had feelings of inadequacy as a teenager. They led her to believe that she was the "ugly duckling" of her senior class. If she only had tanned skin... if she only weighed less... if she only had better looks... if she only had more of this or more of that, she reasoned. These deficiencies bothered her greatly and she would literally spend hours in front of the bathroom mirror cursing them, one by one.

Mary remembers thinking about Hans Christian Andersen's classic tale, *The Ugly Duckling*, and how the appeal of that story lies in its happy ending, when the ugly duckling turns into a beautiful swan!

But who or what could make her beautiful? Where was her magic lantern... her genie... Did she get three wishes?

No doubt you have felt the same way. You, too, have looked in the mirror and wished that you were someone else... someone beautiful... someone attractive... someone—

just anyone—but you!

Yes, we're all presumin' that we could be kind of human if we only had a change.

Like Dorothy and her three companions, we find ourselves waiting for an audience with the Wizard of Oz. Announced by one of his guards, we too begin to imagine dreamily the changes such a visit will bring. Our hope is best expressed by the Cowardly Lion when he boasts, "In another hour I'll be King of the forest .... Long live the King!"

And who is this Wizard we've come to expect so much from? Or more accurately, who are these wizards? In contemporary terms, they are the wizards of status, success, money, power, and prestige. They are the wizards that come on late night TV and entice us with real-estate scams, get-rich-quick schemes, and body and face makeover products. They promise us success and happiness if we follow their yellow brick road of advice—their few, simple, easy (but expensive) steps to fame and fortune, better health, long life, thinness, and a body beautiful. True contentment at last!

Some wizards are relatively harmless—like pop-psychologist Dr. Psycho-Babble and her "abracadabra" formula for better living; or televangelist Rev. Cheap Grace and his so-called "Gospel of Prosperity"; or world renowned author and lecturer Professor Know-it-all and her seven-step method to having your cake and eating it too.

Other wizards are not so harmless—like the wizards of drugs, alcohol, and sex. They prey upon our human weaknesses and destructive dependencies. They promise us painless escape, appealing to an amusement park mentality—but bringing destruction, guilt, shame, and remorse instead. With them, we are never better off. Each time we take their advice we die—-a little at a time, until we are no more.

In *The Wizard of Oz*, Dorothy and her travel companions will soon learn that being great and all-powerful is not synonymous with benevolence and good will. Once in the presence of the Wizard, their hopes will be dashed with the harsh words: "Go away and come back tomorrow .... Now go!" With these words, the Cowardly Lion runs out of the Wizard's chamber and down a long hallway, then jumps through a plate glass window.

You see, the Wizard wasn't what he had expected. Unfortunately, we are affected very much the same way when it comes to our contemporary Wizards of Oz. We go to them expecting so much... and come away disappointed in their often unfeeling, distant, and coarse ways. We feel exploited at times when we discover that it's money, not mission, that motivates so many of our wizards.

Larry, for instance, once had a conversation with a palm reader—certainly, a contemporary wizard—who confided that most people came to her palm reading shop for the brief companionship she could provide. "Why, just think about it," she continued. "Isn't it the warm touch of the hand and a soft caress of the fingers that brings my clients back, again and again, wanting more of the same?" And you know she's right. Even prostitutes tell us that a number of their patrons come, not for sex, but for uninhibited conversation, a listening ear, and unconditional companionship.

Maybe we're not too different. Maybe the changes we seek are prompted more by our need to be accepted, approved, and admired than anything seriously lacking from within.

Jessica, to cite another instance, knew even as a young adult that her feelings of inadequacy often led her to conclude, however falsely, that she was not desirable and that to change herself—either physically, intellectually, or emotionally—might make her more socially acceptable. To be more socially acceptable, she thought, meant being closer to true contentment.

This false notion was later challenged when Jessica's brother became a celebrated young stage actor in a new, off-Broadway musical. "I remember it was opening night," recalled Jessica. "In his dressing room were numerous tokens of admiration that wished him continued success in the years ahead. There, in the center of the room, sat my brother with well-wishers, fellow Thespians, and local reporters. 'How thrilled he must be,' I reasoned. Here he was off to a great start in the theater, with the approval and admiration of both colleagues and peers.

"Once we were alone, I walked up to him and offered my meager congratulations. But as I approached him I noticed he was crying. Well, that made sense—obviously, tears of joy. After all, my brother had arrived. His dream was now coming true. He had followed the formula for theatrical success as prescribed by the Wizards of the Arts and so here he was about to embark on a most promising career.

"But to my surprise the tears were not joyful ones. He was crying because the attention he received was not for who he was but for what he could do. 'If I no longer act,' he concluded, 'then I cease to exist.'"

This feeling of being nothing—like Jessica's brother fearing extinction—must come from somewhere. Certainly, we aren't born with such terrible feelings of inadequacy. Unlike the Scarecrow, the Tin Man, or the Lion, we surely weren't put together without hearts or brains or much-needed courage. Where, then, do such insufferable feelings of despair come from?

Sometimes a dysfunctional home produces family members who feel unaccepted and unloved. But too often the real problem lies in our misperceptions of home. We may perceive it as boring and unfulfilling, when actually it is there where we can find love and acceptance and ultimately our greatest feelings of contentment.

Let's not forget the central figure in *The Wizard of* Oz, Dorothy Gail from Kansas. After all, it is Dorothy who longs to exchange the troubles of this life for new-found adventures over the rainbow. Like many of us today, she believes that by running away to a fantasyland she can find lasting contentment. Yet once Dorothy finds herself over the rainbow, all she keeps telling people is, "I want to go home." Have we found the key? Alex Haley, author of the best-selling book *Roots*, discovered the path that leads to true contentment. "The family is our refuge and springboard," he writes. "Nourished on it, we can advance to new horizons .... In every conceivable manner, the family is link to our past, bridge to our future."

Obviously Peter Collier, well-known author and lecturer, would agree. "Your family," concludes Collier, "is your limits and your possibilities!"

For Dorothy, her family was her refuge—her help in times of trouble. This became clear to her the farther she ventured from home. With the help of Professor Marvel and his crystal ball, she remembered how her Auntie Em had nursed her back to health. "She stayed right by me every minute," she fondly recalled. When locked up in the castle of the Wicked Witch of the West, she would again see her Auntie Em in a crystal ball. This time, helpless Dorothy would again and again cry aloud, "Auntie Em! Come back! Auntie Em?"

It will be our families that either hinder or help. When push comes to shove, we will either run to them in times of trouble or flee—seeking from wizards what only home was originally meant to provide. To put it another way: we will either eventually learn, like Dorothy, to rely on our families for nurture and support or, like Jessica's brother, we will continue to seek from the world what psychologist William

James identifies as the most important need of all—to be appreciated.

WHAT THE WIZARDS OF OZ CAN'T GIVE US

Dr. Richard Klemer, a nationally known family life expert, has painted an interesting psychological landscape of a post-nuclear holocaust society. In the event of such a nuclear war, when the immediate danger is past and it is finally deemed safe to come out of hiding, Klemer suggests that the first thing most people will do is search for their families. Such observations remind us that the family is more important than we realize.

Prominent family scholar Dr. Nick Stinnett agrees. He writes, "We have considerable evidence that the quality of family life is extremely important to our emotional well-being, our happiness, and our mental health as individuals."[1] Did you know, for example, that poor relationships in the family are very strongly related to many of the problems in society, such as juvenile delinquency? It's true.

But for the many dysfunctional families in our world today, there are an equal if not greater number of functional families that exhibit a high degree of marital happiness and good parent-child relationships.

These families do much for their members in positive and productive ways. Unfortunately we don't hear much about

[1] Nick Stinnett, Barbara Chesser and John DeFrain, eds. *Building Family Strengths: Blueprints for Action* (Lincoln, NE: University of Nebraska Press, 1974), 23.

them, do we? Instead, our world takes its cue from such negative role models as television's Ewings, Carringtons, and Bundys! If these families really did represent the best our world had to offer, surely no one would click her heels, like Dorothy did, and say, "There's no place like home."

But these healthy families do exist—all over America. They can provide their members with far more than all the Wizards of Oz put together.

What is it that our families can give us that the Wizards of Oz can't? Consider the following: according to the world's experts, the family provides its members with intimacy, security, protection, caring relationships, and a sense of belonging. Certainly, such things can never be found in any wizard's black bag. Isn't that ultimately the lesson Dorothy learned?

But part of the lesson Dorothy will learn is a painful one. Like many of us, Dorothy is confronted with the reality that things aren't always what they seem to be. Even the people we admire most—and go to for counsel and advice—can disappoint us when we discover how human and how much like the rest of us they really are.

How disappointed Dorothy must have been when, to her absolute surprise, the self-proclaimed "great and powerful" Wizard of Oz turned out to be less than she expected. When Toto snatched away the Wizard's velvet veil, Dorothy suddenly saw her all-powerful Wizard was just a man, after all. Truth is often stranger than fiction, and the disappointment of many Americans was as real as Dorothy's—as the Totos of this world draw back the curtains on a number of self-proclaimed "wizards"—men like Jim Bakker, Jimmy Swaggart, and one-time presidential hopeful Gary Hart. In the words of the Wizard of Oz himself, "It's not that [we're] bad person[s], you understand... it's just that [we're] very bad wizard[s]." How true!

Perhaps the most revealing comment made by the Wizard of Oz is heard during his feeble attempt to take Dorothy home. As the balloon is accidentally dislodged, Dorothy cries aloud, "Please come back! Don't leave Oz without me!"

"I can't," confesses the Wizard, "I don't know how it works!" Even the Wizard, for all his good intentions, is powerless to bring Dorothy home. Shattered, Dorothy begins to weep. "Now I'll never get home."

"Stay with us then, Dorothy, we all love you," consoles the Lion. Dorothy realizes, however, that Oz can never be like home. Missing her family now more than ever before, it is here that Dorothy's greatest lesson is learned—a valuable lesson about home.

Three

Dorothy Goes Home

Just when Dorothy is about to give up, Glenda, the Good Witch of the North appears. "Here's someone who can help you," says the Scarecrow. However, the Scarecrow is only partially correct. Although Glenda does offer help, it's really Dorothy, we are told, who has always had the power to go home.

"Then why didn't you tell her?" the Scarecrow asks. "Because," says Glenda, "she wouldn't have believed me; she had to learn it for herself."

"What have you learned, Dorothy?" asks the Tin Man.

"Well, I think that it wasn't enough just to want to see Uncle Henry and Auntie Em... and... that if I ever go looking for my own heart's desire again, I won't look any further than my own backyard; because if it isn't there, I never really lost it to begin with."

"Is that it?" Dorothy asks Glenda.

"That's all it is."

With this revelation, Dorothy kisses her friends good-bye and, following Glenda's instructions, she clicks her heels three times and says, "There's no place like home... there's no place like home... there's no place like home."

With Auntie Em's voice softly calling to Dorothy to wake up, she begins to slip back into consciousness — back home again, in Kansas!

LOOKING NO FURTHER THAN YOUR OWN BACKYARD

Dorothy's return to consciousness brings to mind the instance of Carlisa, who remembers the time when her precious son, Patrick—then only eight years old—had slipped into a coma due to spinal meningitis.

Fearing the worst, she assembled her family together to offer prayers on his behalf. Even the doctors were skeptical, and it looked like Patrick might never return to this world. Determined to not give up, Carlisa recorded the voices of family members. Some read books, others poems or lyrics to songs. These recorded messages were then played on a small cassette player on the night stand near Patrick's bed. Over and over again as he lay unconscious, Patrick's family called to him through his cloudy subconscious state. "It was my mother's voice, Patrick's grandmother, that eventually called my son back from the brink of death."

Tears flooding her eyes, Carlisa concluded: "When the doctors and medicines failed us, our own family came through. It was as though we had been allowed to experience this painful ordeal to learn that it would be the members of our own household who could eventually accomplish what everyone else was powerless to do."

So we watch as Dorothy is pulled from fantasy back to reality by the loving presence of both family and friends. With Dorothy's dream now over, her journey of hope ends with these simple but powerful words:

> *Toto, we're home... home.*
> *And this is my room.*
> *And you're all here.*
>   *And I'm not going to leave here,*
> *ever, ever again.*
> *Because I love you all;*
> *And, oh, Auntie Em ....*
> *There's no place like home.*

WHEN YOU'RE HOME AND YOU DON'T EVEN KNOW IT

Yes, Dorothy's right—"There's no place like home." That's the lesson she learned over the rainbow and ultimately the lesson we all must learn—especially those who have yet to return from Oz, those whose lives are still held captive in the castle of the Wicked Witch of the West.

Bill, for instance, was sitting alone in his hotel room waiting until it was time to go to the local night club to perform his stand-up comedy routine. Bored, he decided to watch TV. As fate would have it, Bill's favorite childhood movie was on—*The Wizard of Oz*. The message of that movie never really caught his attention before. But now alone, Bill began to think about the choices he had made. He thought about his career and of how he had allowed it to become more important than his role as father and husband. He thought about his three children and of how much he missed them. Thinking about his wife, he began to cry. "Why am I here in this hotel room all alone?" he pondered. "What am I looking for? Where am I going?"

Like Dorothy, Bill has always had the power to go home. But why didn't he? If Bill could tell you, he'd say that he is following his own yellow brick road, seeking to receive from the world what only his family can provide. But Bill doesn't feel secure in his role as father and husband. He feels like a failure because he thinks he doesn't have the brains or the courage or perhaps even the heart to give his family what they need. You see, Bill came from a broken home. His dad was too busy for him, and the skills and insights he would normally have received from his father's role modeling were conspicuously absent in his adult life. Bill is continuing the cycle. And yet he feels a void. He wants to go home, but he thinks he doesn't have the power. But he does.

Yes, that's the message. You can go home. Right now. As the hymn rightfully proclaims: "Softly and tenderly Jesus is calling.... Come home, come home.... Ye who are weary, come home."

God empowers us to make the journey home, not with three clicks of our heels or the reciting of five magical words, but by his power that is at work within us. Returning to God is the first step toward home. As our lives are made right with him, all other relationships begin to fall into place. He breaks the cycle and lays a new foundation upon which our restored home is to be built. Our intimacy with him creates true and lasting intimacy with others. A restoration of heart brings a restoration of home.

This is where The Oz Syndrome ends and lasting peace and contentment begin. It is then that we finally learn, as did Dorothy, that life's greatest treasures are, indeed, closer than we think. "Command those who are... in this present world not... to put their hope in [that] ... which is so uncertain, but to put their hope in God, who richly provides us with every-thing .... In this way they will lay up treasure for themselves as a firm foundation for the coming age, so that they may take hold of the life that is truly life" (1 Tim. 6:17-19).

Part Two

The Obstacles of Oz: The Problem

Before Dorothy discovers the true significance and sacredness of home, she—as we—must first confront the obstacles of Oz. She must run the gauntlet through a series of problems that make the comfort and safety of home so attractive. Contentment does not come without trials, nor without price.

Part Two looks at these obstacles in an attempt to define the problems before Parts Three and Four counter them with other values *and offer solutions. Chapter 4 uncovers the various spirits of Oz—and the world—that haunt us individually: spirits of egotism, materialism, escapism, and defeatism. Chapter 5 narrows in on troubled families as a major obstacle to contentment.*

Four

The Spirits of Oz

Who can forget that wonderful song as sung by the Munchkins, "Ding Dong, the Witch is Dead?" What a great feeling it must have been for those little Munchkins to have the Wicked Witch of the East completely annihilated with one neat drop of a house. Why, in the blink of an eye, their once-powerful and most deadly foe was wiped out. "Now you see it .... Now you don't!" What a marvelous stroke of good Munchkin fortune!

One of the Munchkins makes a proclamation: "This is a

day of independence for all the Munchkins and their descendants!" What a wise choice of words, for the Munchkins are indeed now free.

Although there is ultimately another witch to contend with, the crushing of the first paves the way for the melting of the second. Such, it seems, is the way of life. No sooner do we eliminate one nasty and destructive habit or foe than another rears its ugly head, often "worse than the first." But if we can crush one, why not melt the other? It's just that simple. But it is really a matter of first identifying those haunting spirits before we can take them out of our lives, one by one. Let's name and tackle them, moving from least to greatest, shall we?

THE SPIRIT OF EGOTISM

"Pride goes before destruction, a haughty spirit before a fall," says wise King Solomon (Prov. 16:18). This little nasty known as pride—egotism—is a real pain in the neck! Try as we might to avoid its lying snare, this spirit would have us believe that we are somehow better than other people—even those in our own household. Such is merely an unrealistic appraisal of who we really are. Thinking more highly of ourselves than we should, we repel people—even the ones we love most—pointing them 180 degrees in the opposite direction.

As with any spirit, the power of the spirit of egotism lies in its ability to deceive. Sometimes that deception can be so cleverly disguised that it takes a trained therapist to detect it. But it doesn't always take an expert to discern even the most hidden habits of the heart. Here's a description of the spirit of egotism and how best to "drop a house" on it.

Characterized by excessive self-absorption, this spirit is answerable to no one. It's a "free spirit." Moving without restraint, it goes where it pleases—and God help anyone who gets in its way! Totally in control, this specter masters its own destiny. Its goal is to convince you to be a free spirit, too. It preys especially on persons who are discontent with their own inadequacies but who deny any imperfection in their lives. Like the spirit haunting them, they build a castle around themselves to protect their inner child from present-day feelings of low self-esteem—often produced by a formerly traumatic and intolerable childhood environment. The spirit of egotism lies to them with thoughts like, "It's okay to be selfish; after all, you've suffered enough at the hands of unusually cruel parents. Total freedom is the only legitimate response to such an unloving parental hell." The castle they erect is in stark contrast to their own vulnerability. Unlike how they truly feel, it is out of proportion to its surroundings, dwarfing and rendering as ordinary everything that falls into its monstrous shadow. It is a frightening fortress, built to scare off anyone who seeks to get too close.

The result is a person who has a self-centered existence and an unquenchable thirst for glory. It's a spell that feeds the imagination with an overinflated sense of self-importance. Visions of grandeur... of conquering... of becoming number one preoccupy our time. Soon, winning at any cost becomes our soul's obsession .... No matter who gets hurt .... No matter who gets pushed away. We simply *must* succeed! Armed with a witch's broomstick, we soar to the top of a malignantly narcissistic existence only to find that it is the spirit of egotism, and not ourselves, enthroned there!

It is then that we realize that "dropping a house" on it is our only means of escape. But to do this "completely and so neatly," we must fill our lives with something other than "a myriad mix of subconscious defense mechanisms designed to protect our deep-rooted insecurity from public exposure."[1] In his book, *Self-Esteem*, Dr. Robert Schuller describes for us how subtly this wicked web of egotism is woven and how it ultimately affects our relationship with God:

1   We withdraw from a belief in God for fear that our sins will be exposed, and we cannot stand the prospect of being embarrassed. So, doubt becomes an early defense mechanism of a non-trusting, guilty soul.

2   Since we are unable to throw off our natural religious instincts, we fabricate our own images of God. As insecure people, our natural fears take the face and form and force of anger. We appear to be mean [the exterior of the castle that we've talked about], but

---

[1] Robert H. Schuller, *Self-Esteem: The New Reformation* (Waco, TX: Word Incorporated, 1982), 66.

actually we are afraid. No wonder then that the unsaved human being imagines God to be angry rather than loving. The tangled web [of the spirit of egotism] is becoming more complex.

3. We withdraw even further from a God [we] picture as a threatening rather than a redeeming figure. The name of the true God of mercy who longs to save his children is not taken seriously.

4 We project these same patterns of human behavior to our other interpersonal relationships. Since we dare not trust, we lie [as the spirit has lied to us]. We are dishonest, lest our imperfections be revealed.[2]

The death blow to such a spirit is the God-honoring proclamation, "Your will, not mine, be done!" Rather than fear God, we embrace his "perfect love" that "casteth out fear" (1 John 4:18). In the presence of such fearless love, we are free to examine our destructive habits of the heart and confess them to God who "is faithful and just and will forgive us our sins and purify us from all unrighteousness" (1 John 1:9). (A more complete discussion of turning to God will be examined in Part Four.)

2 Schuller, 66.

THE SPIRIT OF MATERIALISM

If ever there was a wicked spirit indigenous to North America, the spirit of materialism is it. How relentlessly we Americans seek the good life with its selfish accumulation of things! Extravagant and luxurious living is the hope held out by this mistress of the dark. Oh, how attractive is this cunning spirit! We covet its emphasis on the sun and sea with bigness and mobility.... Ah, take the plunge.... Go for it .... You only live once! Delayed gratification is to be spurned. We want it now! "Why, it's a sign of weakness," it lies. "The true measure of a man or woman is in the abundance of their possessions .... Yes, to the victors belong the spoils.... The person with the most toys at the end of his or her life wins!"

The problem with this bourgeois spirit of materialism is its focus on the wrong kind of treasure. It fails to acknowledge the possibility that there exists something more valuable than things.

As a young adolescent, for instance, Sally stayed at a friend's house most waking hours of the day. This seemed peculiar to her parents, who had provided her with the most attractive family room money could buy—state-of-the-art stereo, TV, VCR, and pool table. What more could Sally possibly want? Still it was Sally's choice to be at her best friend's house in one of the worst parts of town,

Little was attractive about the simple, two-story townhouse that lacked most modern conveniences. For Sally, though, there was something more to that humble abode than met the eye. It was there that Sally felt an unexplainable contentment and the very real feeling of being more important than things. "They had so little, my friend and her mother, but they had each other," Sally confided. "You could tell that each was the other's treasure. And that's how that house—my friend and her mother—made me feel, too."

Sally could tell you that "dropping a house" on this spirit of materialism begins with the attitude that relationships—especially in a family—and not collectibles are what really matter. This is something her parents have yet to figure out!

Bill and Francis, to cite another instance, lost their daughter to a rare childhood disease. A year after their tragedy, Bill was visiting a friend who shared that he, too, had lost a child. The friend put his hand on Bill's shoulder and spoke a profound truth, "Now we both have treasures in heaven."

All of a sudden the words of Jesus began to make sense to this once despairing father: "Do not store up for yourselves treasures on earth, where moth and rust destroy, and where thieves break in and steal. But store up for yourselves treasures in heaven, where moth and rust do not destroy, and where thieves do not break in and steal. For where your treasure is, there your heart will be also" (Matt. 6:19-21). "Wow, I finally understand," sighed Bill. "I finally understand."

Oh, if we could only get a handle on what Bill has learned

and on what is being communicated from God to us. Yes, we could hold a key that unlocks a door to true and lasting contentment. It's the simplest yet most difficult concept for North Americans to grasp. You see, we are honestly not equipped to handle such truth. Its implications elude us. Its real meaning escapes us. We look... but do not see. We hear... but do not understand. We read... but miss the point entirely. *How truly bewitched we are!*

Sally takes it to heart. She makes the right choice by learning from her friend's family. But many of us do not. We have been beguiled by a spirit of materialism that will not let us go. It keeps us forever at arm's length with one tactical plan: fear of the unknown.

Let's be honest. We fear what tomorrow may bring. We read in the local newspaper of life's uncertainties. Radio and TV haunt us with a steady drone of messages that remind how vulnerable we really are. Here one minute, gone the next is a creepy, unsettling thought, to be sure. Oh, how temporary life is!

Fear soon gives birth to worry. We become anxious for tomorrow, don't we? Then those devilish "what if's" appear— the scary offspring of the spirit of materialism. They taunt us with, "what if you don't have enough food to eat?" or "what if there is not enough water to drink?" or—perish the thought— "what if there is nothing to wear?"

We become obsessed with the things we eat, drink, and wear. We sow, reap, and store away in large malls all such necessities. When fear grips us, we simply scramble into our cars and drive to that part of town "where troubles melt like lemon drops" and "clouds are far behind me." We follow the yellow brick road... to the local shopping mall. But remember, the song "Somewhere Over the Rainbow" is a reminder of life's bitter limitations: "Birds fly over the rainbow," concludes Dorothy. "Why then, oh why, can't I?"

Speaking of birds, God has a lot to say about them. His commentary on the life of birds becomes just the house we need to drop on this materialistic mistress of the mall. Whether or not birds fly over the rainbow is of no particular interest to Jesus. What is of interest to him is our complete trust in him. "Look at the birds of the air; they do not sow or reap or store away in barns, and yet your heavenly Father feeds them. Are you not much more valuable than they? Who of you by worrying can add a single hour to his life?" (Matt. 6:26-27)

Jesus continues his unique teaching on the contented life: And why do you worry about clothes? See how the lilies of the field grow. They do not labor or spin. Yet I tell you that not even Solomon in all his splendor was dressed like one of these. If that is how God clothes the grass of the field, which is here today and tomorrow is thrown into the fire, will he not much more clothe you, O you of little faith? So do not worry, saying, "What shall we eat?" or "What shall we drink?" or "What shall we wear?" For the pagans run after all these things, and your heavenly Father knows that you need them. But seek first his kingdom and his righteousness, and all these things will be given to you as well. Therefore do not worry about tomorrow, for tomorrow will worry about itself (Matt. 6:28-34).

Oh, what wonderful words of *life!* This perspective delivers a death blow to the spirit of materialism. Without fear, without worry, this worldly spirit can no longer enslave us. Free of its deception we are like birds soaring high in the sky, knowing to whom we belong. It will be our roots that set us free—a deeply-rooted contentment with our families and well-grounded faith in God, our heavenly Father. Like the birds of the air, we will be taken care of by his almighty hand and freed to love and be loved. This is buried treasure for some; but for others, it is the pot of gold of human relationships that have their beginning and ultimate fulfillment in God—in his kingdom, his righteousness—where the familial treasures are found.

THE SPIRIT OF ESCAPISM

This spirit is headed for the top of the pop charts, with its media-savvy and cinematic manipulation. It dominates all that is pleasing to the eye and soothing to the ears. This baroque spirit best controls those prone to fantasy games, amusement parks, premieres of highly touted movies, and an eagerness for fleeting pleasures found in drugs, alcohol, and sex. It advocates anything that will take one away from life and all of its small, repetitive, tawdry dreariness.

Basically, the spirit of escapism is bored and it wants you to be, too!

Its castle—like that of the Wicked Witch of the West—is its trap; its facade, the enticing snare. It hides the mundane behind a shroud of tasteless glitter with neon lights and signs that titillate the senses. Like a prostitute whose body is adorned to seduce, its fortress seeks to hold us in its arms and offer temporary escape. But how dark are its inner walls and how terrible its enchanted rooms! It is a place of the damned who, like Dorothy awaiting her doom in the castle of the wicked witch, only then realize that the family stands in the light of a reality more glorious and fair.

How our hearts yearn for our families when they are nowhere in sight. Jesus knew this when he said,

"For where your treasure is, there your heart will be also" (Matt. 6:21).

Lilly had always wanted to buy the old family farm with all of its childhood memories: Mom baking cookies on a rainy Saturday afternoon... Dad in the basement fixing a wagon, with its wheel loose from over-extended play... brother Billy, running feverishly all over the house looking for the hamster that got away.... But to her surprise and absolute despair, the familiar homestead proved a poor substitute in the absence of family and friends.

"I had no sooner purchased the house and land, but that a terrible sense of loneliness and discontentment came over me," Lilly confided.

"Suddenly I found myself understanding that silly, almost incomprehensible line from The Wizard of Oz. Oh, you know the one where she tells Glenda at the end of her journey what she learned. Why, it finally made sense to me—the idea that if I ever go looking for my own heart's desire again, I won't look any further than my own backyard; because if it isn't there, I never really lost it to begin with. Yes, I agree. It's Mom. It's Dad. It's my brother. They are my heart's desire. With them gone, my backyard—regardless of all of its wonderful memories—could never give me what I truly crave. Home is where the heart is. And I'm at home in my heart when in the presence of my family and friends!"

The death blow to this spirit is a return to one's family, with all of its infinite possibilities for intimacy, security, protection, caring relationships, and a sense of belonging. It is a sacred place—no matter how imperfect, no matter its faults. Even with the most strained of human relationships, it is our family, and nothing else that, like our relationship with God, is set apart by the great expectation that it will endure! In this belief, we are at once freed from the evil grasp of the spirit of escapism and delivered into the hands of our family and friends—finally free to contemplate the shortness of this life when compared to eternity with them.

THE SPIRIT OF DEFEATISM

Simply put, the Spirit of Defeatism is a demon of low self-esteem! This one is worse than the first three because it appears to be the foundation for all other hungers of the human spirit. To describe its deceptions is to come close to our own self-loathing—you know, the kind of experience where we look in the mirror and hate what we see.

Such defeatist attitudes are tell-tale signs that this spirit is not lagging far behind us. If we would examine our feelings carefully we would learn that the spirit of defeatism has been hanging around for a long, long time—no doubt, as early as childhood.

This haunting devil knows that you can only give what you've been taught through a lifetime of formal or informal critical life experiences. To be deprived of love is to pave the way for defeat in the most important of all human arenas—interpersonal relationships.

Have you ever habitually protested, "I can't—I know I can't—please don't make me!" Or ever asked someone, over and over again, "Did I do it right?" with a kind of searching-for-approval tone of voice? If so, then it may be that you, too, are under the spell of this bewitching derogation of the soul with its saddest of all human proclamations, "Nobody likes me—absolutely nobody!"

Such statements reflect a fundamental discontentment with self and an inability to face life with pleasurable anticipation. Rather than enjoy life, we fear it. Rather than enjoy others, we fear them! This is a bondage more terrible than any physical prison, because it is a self-imposed hell wherein we are unable to venture far from a vine that produces fruit of inadequacy and guilt. The spirit of defeatism plants such a vine in its efforts to choke the life out of all our God-given potential for human accomplishment.

By contrast, Jesus simply states, "'Love the Lord your God with all your heart and with all your soul and with all your strength and with all your mind'; and, 'Love your neighbor as yourself'" (Luke 10:27).

Such truth strips our old nemesis of her defeatist powers by affirming loudly and clearly that we can only love others to the extent to which we love ourselves; that self-love is a divine, albeit much distorted key ingredient in human dignity which ultimately flows from a right relationship with God!

To "drop a house" on this spirit we must embrace—with all our heart, soul, mind, and might—the security of being one of God's children whom he loves and delivers from evil. This is the only legitimate antidote for our fears! In the presence of God, we become immune to the spirit's ridicule. We now throw off its labels of "stupid," "ugly," "failure," and the like, and instead embrace the liberating truth that we are made in the image of God, with all his capacity to be patient, kind, protective, trusting, hopeful, and persevering. We are now freed to love others as we have been truly loved!

LOVE YOUR FAMILY AS YOU LOVE YOURSELF

Religious men have asked, "Who is my neighbor?" Jesus' response is profound—and not for the reasons most of us would think! To be sure, Jesus was dealing with our prejudices and our inability to love neighbors of different races and different cultures. But what for me is even more significant is the connection of the Greek word "neighbor" with its synonym "blood relative." "Neighbor" to the Greek mind had more to do with kinship and conjugal relationships than geographical proximity. One's neighbors could actually be one's relatives. When seen from this vantage point, we realize loving one's neighbor begins at home! Jesus might well have said, "Love your family—your wife or husband or kids or anyone you're related to by blood—as you love yourself." Now that's profound!

I mention this because I believe that the ultimate house to drop on the spirits just examined is our own house. Consider Dorothy who dropped her family's house on the Wicked Witch of the East. Remember? Well, that's what we should do.

But to do this we have to go home. Yes, we have to go home—back over the rainbow—to the only people who really matter in this life. And we've got to learn to love them as we love ourselves. To do this, however, requires God's help. We dare not make the journey alone. Without God and his ability to change our lives through the power of his Holy Spirit we might, like Lilly, whose story is illustrated above, return to an empty house. And the spirits in our way don't fear empty houses—no, not really—just houses filled with families and friends, where we loudly proclaim, as did Dorothy, "You're all here.., and oh... there's no place like home!" Coming home from Oz, we can find, as Dorothy found, true contentment in the sacredness of the family.

Five

Families in Trouble

Many families today are not the safe havens that we might wish for. They should be and could be, but realistically, many American families are in trouble these days. They represent a different obstacle than those detailed in the last chapter. Families in trouble are in a kind of bondage or oppression, but we can learn to liberate them by more closely examining Dorothy's experiences in Oz.

The importance of families cannot be overestimated. In almost every survey I looked at, the greater percentage of people said family ties are the most important part of their lives. Surveys conducted over half a century by more than a dozen research organizations confirm that Americans say family life is more important than work, recreation, money, or even friendships.

A 1989 Gallup poll, for example, found "a good family life" ranked first in importance for nearly nine out of ten Americans—89 percent! Add to that the many studies conducted between 1970-1988 which found a connection between having a satisfactory family life and having a contented life in general.[1]

Apparently the problem is that *we don't practice what we preach*!

Although we say we place a high value on family life and that family life is our greatest source of contentment, it is still not unusual for a person to sacrifice family for largely materialistic goals such as financial or career success. *So what's going on?*

Well, some family life experts say self-interest is replacing family interest, even to the extent that it is competing with family commitment and parenting.[2] I couldn't agree more.

And nowhere do I see this focus on self-interest more evident than among young males between the ages of eighteen and twenty-two, who believe that self-fulfillment

[1] "The Family Values of Americans," Wing Spread Commission on the Family in America, (Institute for American Values Working Paper, no. wp7, 1991).

[2] James A. Sweet and Larry L. Bumpass, *American Families and Households* (New York: Russell Sage Foundation, 1987).

comes with great financial reward. It's as though they feel a restlessness until they acquire their first million. Of course, the probability of acquiring a million in their lifetime becomes remote, and the fear of financial calamity forces many to contemplate illegal and unethical business actions.

It isn't enough to talk to these young men about all that focusing on their families could provide. As I will explain in chapter 11, we must first move them toward God.

If I were to ask you to consider historical events that signified the liberating of people from political, economic, or even religious oppression, dates such as 1787 might come to mind with the Bill of Rights, or 1776 with the signing of the Declaration of Independence, or even as recently as 1990 with the fall of communism. Probably not mentioned would be 1939, when, in the MGM movie version of *The Wizard of* Oz, Dorothy "liquidates" the Wicked Witch of the West with a bucket of water or drops a house on the Wicked Witch of the East in Munchkin County of the land called Oz.

And that's okay, really. No history professor would expect you to list Dorothy as one of the great liberators of the Western world. But in a symbolic sense, that's exactly what she did: liberate Munchkins, Winkie Guards, and Winged Monkeys from the tyranny of an oppressive and undesirable dictatorship. With one drop of a house and one toss of a pail she unintentionally changed the entire course of a mythical lineage of dwarfs, witches, and wizards. Wow! That's a tad bit more than I've ever done.

It may be interesting to return to Oz to see how this formerly abusive and emotionally destructive environment has changed. As far as we know, even the Wizard himself is off floating around somewhere—caught between the fantasyland of Oz and the earthly reality of Kansas. Instead of a dictatorship, even the Emerald City is enjoying as close to a democratic system as you can get with a lion, tin woodsman, and scarecrow operating by consensus.

When you really think about it, Dorothy did liberate a lot of people in a short period of time. Her contribution to Oz was to take the destructiveness out of its legacy so that future generations would have the guidance of the Scarecrow—"by virtue of his superior brain"; the Lion—"by virtue of his courage"; and the Tin Man—"by virtue of his magnificent heart"—to help them build new and productive lives.

Let's concentrate for a moment on Dorothy as the "Great Emancipator" and begin to think how we might join her in a quest to seek out and liberate families in a strange land.

LIBERATING FAMILIES:
THE WICKED WITCH IS DEAD!

While in the castle of the Wicked Witch of the West, Dorothy had time to re-examine her priorities. As death loomed close, she realized family mattered more than ever as she was forced to watch an hourglass mark her remaining moments alive.

This scene is actually quite terrifying—especially for the 1930s. In it, we really get to see just how wicked the Wicked Witch is. With little concern for a young girl's anguish, the Witch even mocks her pain and her Auntie Em—whom Dorothy desperately calls out to in a moment of fear and desperation.

It's unfortunate that, when watching this movie with certain friends, this particular scene seems to conjure up early childhood experiences that are quite painful. Usually these memories involve a mother or father; maybe a mom or dad; in some cases even an adopted or foster parent. Whatever the case, the memories are difficult to deal with because they involve people of great influence and control in our lives. They are persons we trust.

The principal caretakers in our young lives play a unique and unparalleled role for either good or evil. With them we are either *bonded* in a family of satisfaction and love or placed in *bondage* within a family of disappointment and abuse.

The latter seems to best describe the inhabitants of the castle of the Wicked Witch of the West.

Who can forget when Dorothy accidentally melts the Witch? It is one of the high points of the movie, if you ask me. Remember that curious last look from Toto as he claws at the place where the Wicked Witch has died? All of sudden one Winkie Guard looks up at Dorothy and says, "You've killed her."

"I didn't mean to kill anyone," Dorothy says in her own

defense. Then to our utter delight, the guard shouts: "Hail Dorothy, the Wicked Witch is dead!" Relief and rejoicing fill the corridors of the once oppressive halls of the Witch's domain. Dorothy is hailed as hero once again.

This new freedom from bondage that Dorothy brought about can be won within a family by forgiveness and by prudent legislation.

FREEDOM BY FORGIVENESS

Now that the Wicked Witch is dead the Winkie Guards and Winged Monkeys, like the Munchkins before them, are free. In response, they sing a new "Battle Hymn of the Republic": "Ding! Dong! The Witch is Dead!" Like their once oppressed little friends, they declare: "This is a day of independence, for all of us and our descendants .... Yes, let the joyous news be spread: the Wicked old Witch at last is dead!"

So goes life in the merry land of Oz.

Yet when talking to some of my friends, I am told that oppressed is exactly how they felt growing up. One young woman said, 'Trapped' is the word that really describes my adolescent experience—every day I found myself threatening to run away and never come back, but then I would just stay and take some more."

Sadly, even as an adult (and now with children of her own), she continues to go home only to be overpowered, abused, and trapped once again.

At this point, I could concentrate the rest of this book on the seriousness of such abuse in our homes, whether it be verbal, physical, sexual, or emotional. I could talk about those who oppress—such as evil dictators, domineering parents, or even wicked witches—and explain how some abusers are really addicted to power at the cost of denigrating others. I could explore with you how those who oppress and those who are oppressed become entwined in a pathology often intergenerational in nature: "like father, like son," etc. I could even go on to provide an adaptation of the Twelve Step Recovery Program of Alcoholics Anonymous (AA), founded in 1934.

But I won't. My focus instead will be on forgiveness.

Forgiveness is the simple yet divine act of letting go, then coming back. It is something Dorothy did. It is an escape, for a time, from that which hurts and a returning with a new inner strength and a new resolve that acknowledges no matter how bad, no matter how flawed, "*There's no place like home.*" It is a relinquishing of all that is past and an embracing of a new-found freedom that comes when we finally learn to forgive.

What is forgiveness? "Forgive" is defined in a dictionary as: "To cease to feel resentment against (an offender) ....' Notice the emphasis on both *feelings* and *ceasing.* This simple definition captures two fundamental tasks. One task is to give up—that is, relinquish past hurts, fears, and anger. The other task is to acknowledge that we do feel hurt, and in

69

some instances, experience that hurt on a daily basis. Giving up such recurring feelings of hurt can never be easy. For those still over the rainbow, returning home to face those feelings with the hope of giving them up permanently may seem an impossible task.

But according to Dr. Grace Ketterman, it can and must occur if the bondage of past abuse is to be broken. She writes:

> Many people I know seem to believe that forgiveness is a simple statement based on an often flimsy decision. The forgiveness I am describing is not that shallow. It begins, in fact, with the acknowledgment of pain. Many victims of... abuse have grown calloused—understandably so.
>
> People can absorb only so much pain and then they will deny it, ignore it, and hide it away in the depths of their memories— a process referred to as repression. It seems less painful to rationalize away the hurts, feel angry, or even worse, indifferent, toward the abuser.
>
> Such efforts to deal with pain, however, are like putting a tiny Band-Aid on a big boil or abscess. In order to heal such an infected wound, the poison must be drained, allowing wholeness to be restored from the inside. So to even begin this healing process of forgiving others demands admitting the

[3] Grace Ketterman, *Verbal Abuse: Healing the Hidden Wound* (Ann Arbor, MI: Servant Publications, 1992), 219–220.

hurt, and in some degree, even reliving it.[3]

Together with the above observations, Dr. Ketterman offers a four-step procedure that encompasses vital stages of forgiveness which has repeatedly brought "inside-out" healing to abuse victims with whom she has worked. These steps are:

1   Acknowledge and face the pain all over again.
2   Collect as much information as possible about the abusive episodes from your past.
3   Allow the information to penetrate to your very heart.
4   Make a conscious choice, by an act of your will, to totally relinquish all the hurts, fears, and anger of the past.[4]

In her own bed, with family and friends all about her, Dorothy began to let go of the pain of being misunderstood. I think, too, that Dorothy had experienced an element of comparison—that is, being over the rainbow (separated from everything familiar to her) was worse than home had ever been.

No matter how hard it may be to hear, *we need our families*—even when they fail us so miserably, hurt us so unfairly, and push us away so unintentionally.

In many ways, this process reminds me of how we are

[4] Ketterman, 222.

with God.

Paul the Apostle, speaking for all of humanity, says: "For I have the desire to do what is good, but I cannot carry it out ....The evil I do not want to do—this I keep on doing. What a wretched man am I!... Who will rescue me?... Thanks be to God—through Jesus Christ our Lord" (Rom. 7:18- 25).

Here's how we break the cycle of abuse and end the evil our families do not want to do. It begins with us. When we do not give up on them but instead show them "the most excellent way" of "love that is patient.., not easily angered... [keeping] no record of wrongs" (1 Cor. 13:4-5), we break the cycle of oppression and bondage to the past. Only as we have been forgiven by Christ can we forgive others (see Matt. 6:12). Is that not the very heart and soul of The Lord's Prayer?

Schuller would agree. Listen, now, to his wise and persuasive words:

> Even as we experience the Lord's forgiving grace when we experience his acceptance of us as imperfect persons, we are now called to accept ourselves, too, as imperfect persons. Then we must move on to transfer this divine grace by accepting others with their imperfections. In doing so, we will be saved from the negative emotions of resentment.[5]

This is the true Emancipation Proclamation: "Our Father in heaven.... Forgive us our debts, as we also have forgiven

[5] Robert H. Schuller, Self-Esteem: The New Reformation (Waco, TX: Word Incorporated, 1982), 50.

our debtors" (Matt. 6:9,12). In this prayer, we experience grace—amazing grace! And we claim our freedom in Christ to give up the past with its bitter resentment and to release, by forgiving as we have been forgiven, those still held in bondage to it. As we liberate our hearts, we liberate our homes and allow our family members—even those who once hurt us—to experience grace; the same grace we have experienced in God.

The conclusion of the matter, however, comes with a warning. Satan, like all wicked witches, will desire bondage for us and our families again. Therefore we must stand our ground and fortify our families against his relentless attacks by continuing to forgive and be forgiven. To this regard, Charles Swindoll cautiously concludes:

I would love to tell you that change is easy, but I cannot. Old habits are terribly difficult to break. Thinking correctly takes courage. Furthermore, our adversary, Satan, won't back off easily.... If you think the plantation slave owners following the Civil War were determined to keep their slaves, I'm here to tell you that today's grace killers are even more stubborn than they were. Count on it, the enemies of our souls despise this message of freedom. They hate grace, so be warned. In order for you to leave the security of slavery and ignorance and walk out into the new, risky fields of freedom and grace, you will need courage and inner resolve. My prayer is that God will give you an abundance of both. You are not alone in your quest for freedom. There are a lot of us taking this journey with you. There is a grace awakening beginning in the hearts of God's people.

Such a warning is necessary. Who knows what battles you will encounter now that you have determined to live emancipated rather than enslaved? But the good news for many is this: At least we have gotten the harpoon into the monster [or thrown water into the face of the Witch]. Now we must steer carefully and watch out for that wicked tail.[6]

FREEDOM BY LEGISLATION

There is another avenue to freedom besides forgiveness. It is freedom by legislation. In an article for the Scripps Howard News Service in 1990, Professor Richard Caldwell constructed a chart that speaks about differences between the values of the 1950s and the 1990s. It is my belief that such values are dramatically changing and will partially account for certain trends that will ultimately incapacitate the family— making it difficult for it to be a stabilizing force in contemporary society.

Many of these value shifts reflect changes in public policy—legislation that often reflects changes in Americans' current lifestyles and value systems.

Where do such shifts in values come from? This is a complex question with more than one answer, but a frequent

[6] Charles Swindoll, *The Grace Awakening* (Dallas: Word Publishing, 1990), 121-122.

response is "future shock" and the adaptability of Americans to an ever-advancing technological age. It's just how we cope, some say, or how we comply with our rapidly changing world. Others suggest it's simply an issue of convenience and control. Examine Professor Caldwell's list and see how many of his 90s attributes have continued or accelerated as we move into a new millennium:

1990s	1950s
Spending	Saving
Instant Gratification	Delayed Gratification
Latchkey Kids	Ozzie & Harriet
Ambivalence	Certainty
Skepticism	Orthodoxy
Leveraging	Investing
Lifestyle	Neighborhood
Underclass	Middle Class
Import	Export
Personal Well-being	Public Virtue
Nanny/Child Care	Mom & Dad
Photo Opportunity	Press Conference
Fame	Achievement
Credential	Knowledge
Service	Manufacturing
Divorce	Duty
"Me"	"We"

"Speed, hyper-speed, and a near obsession with convenience, flexibility, tangibility, options, quality, short-term commitments, and individualism characterize the designer lifestyles of the fast-lane 1990s," said Russell Chandler, former religion specialist for *The Los Angeles Times.* "Above all, we want to stay in control."[7] He concluded that with the world's population being urbanized, and natural units like the family breaking down, many of our so called "traditional" values are on the way out.

The issue for me, then, is what concern (if any) should our government have about values and the role they play in American family life? Are there ideals, for example, that ought to be supported by Washington as foundational to family survival? In a democratic republic, do we dare affirm that certain values are important and indispensable or simply a matter for individual conscience to decide?

Obviously Dorothy brought values to Oz that reflected her Judeo-Christian heritage. "Why, you shouldn't go around picking on things weaker than you are!" she scolds the Cowardly Lion. Sure sounds like a moralist to me! And when we watch the film as family, we agree with her, don't we? These are the timeless values that we treasure that are sometimes hidden in *The Wizard of Oz*. Should they be preserved?

Many of us have watched with disappointment the modern-day cartoon versions of *The Wizard of Oz*. They are sometimes so radical, so contrary to traditional values that we can barely stomach one episode. We tell our kids, "That's not *The Wizard of Oz* I remember!" Is MGM's *The Wizard of Oz* worth remembering? Is there a part of Americana reflected in the movie that we long to return to? I think the answer is,

[7] Russell Chandler, *Racing Toward 2000* (Grand Rapids, MI: Harper Collins/ Zondervan, 1991), 82.

"Yes!"

Obviously, Gary L. Bauer, a domestic policy advisor during the Reagan administration and former undersecretary of the U.S. Department of Education, agrees. In a public policy paper entitled "The Family: Preserving America's Future," he offered the following recommendation:

> It is time to reaffirm some "home truths" and to restate the obvious. Intact families are good. Families who choose to have children are making a desirable decision. Mothers and fathers who then decide to spend a good deal of time raising those children themselves, rather than leaving it to others, are demonstrably doing a good thing for those children. Countless Americans do these things every day. They ask for no special favors—they do these things naturally out of love, loyalty and a commitment to the future. They are the bedrock of our society. Public policy and the culture in general must support and reaffirm these decisions—not undermine and be hostile to them or send a message that we are neutral.[8]

Commenting on his own report, Bauer called his recommendation a "celebration of the norm" with "verbal praise of family values." He concluded that "private choices [have] public consequences.... USA *Today* endorsed the report, saying:

> Strong families are the cornerstone of the USA. They play a vital role

[8] James Dobson and Gary L. Bauer, *Children at Risk* (Dallas: Word Incorporated, 1990), 92-93.

in our free society. Federal policies should not ignore or penalize families. Intact families are good....It's a simple message, but one we need to hear.[9]

If Dorothy desired to return home to Kansas, then it's my hope Americans will desire to return to *The Wizard of* Oz to reflect on what drew us to the film in the first place. Certainly the movie's message is a simple one, but one we need to hear again and again.

Every time legislation has a negative impact on the family, remember *The Wizard of* Oz and the simple values of a little girl. Every time we hear of a bill destructive to our homes, remember Dorothy, who learned "The Golden Rule" of doing unto others as you would have them do unto you.

She didn't leave the Scarecrow hanging or the Tin Man wanting or the Lion unassisted with his dreams. She stopped. She listened. And most of all, she cared. These are the timeless values she learned as a child. These are the values that we once knew and practiced and taught—the values most Americans hold dear.

FAMILY VALUES TODAY:
"I DON'T THINK WE'RE IN KANSAS ANYMORE!"

When Dorothy found herself over the rainbow, she was immediately confronted with change. So apparent was the change that she pondered aloud, "Toto, I don't think we're in Kansas anymore." She was right. But unfortunately, that's

[9] "Government Must Strengthen Family," USA *Today* (November 21, 1982), 12A.

how many Americans feel as they look out across their own backyards and see soaring crime rates, frequent abuse of alcohol and other drugs, and the easy availability of guns.

Apparently Dorothy isn't the only one trying to get back home these days. In an unprecedented report, *Time* recently stated that baby boomers are searching for "spiritual homes.[10] "People are in the seeking mode," the article concludes. "Increasing numbers... are turning religious again ...."

Perhaps we've ignored the role traditional values once played in our lives, traditional values that reflected a spiritual heritage allowed and even encouraged in our democratic society. The church was once considered good: millions of families once brought what was considered good about the church back into their homes. There was a time not too long ago when we dared to practice what we preached. Or at least we tried to. But then things began to change.

Now it would appear that change is not always good—especially for families—and that certain values, specifically Christian ones, are worth preserving. *Time* begins its report:

Back in the early 1960s, when cars were big and hair was short and families that prayed together stayed together, the Walceks said grace before meals and went to Mass every single morning. Emil and Kathleen sent their nine children to the local parochial schools in Placentia, California, and on Sunday

[10] "The Church Search," *Time* (April 5, 1993), 44-49.

mornings at St. Joseph's the family took up two pews.

Then one by one, the children set off on their spiritual travels, and in the process perfectly charted the journey of their generation. Emil Jr., 45, and Edward, 32, dropped out of church, and stayed out. John, 43, was married on a cliff overlooking Laguna Beach, divorced—and returned to the Catholic Church, saying, "Maybe the traditional way of doing things isn't so bad."[11]

What I find fascinating is that much of the religious revival happening in America today is fueled by family concerns. Churches, perhaps for the first time, are realizing that they need families, that they need to be family-oriented, or else pay the high cost of membership decline. Churches can no longer try to compete with the family, but instead must seek to strengthen it. If there is truth to the saying, "As the family goes, so goes the nation," then it is equally true that "As the family goes, so goes the church." To strengthen the family is to strengthen the church. Churches are beginning to realize that they are only as strong as their families. Without family as the fundamental unit of society churches may not survive in the twenty-first century.

What is the implication here? Well, let's think about it for a moment.

Time magazine is only partially right. To be sure, millions are now returning to church in ever-increasing numbers. But

---

[11] "The Church Search," 44-45.

why they are returning needs to be explored. *Time's* so called "Church Search" concentrates on the search for spiritual homes, i.e., the church, but fails to acknowledge that our generation is first returning to a more traditional and sacred view of home—with a renewed focus on family—and then searching for a church that will compliment the values once found in our own backyards. *What we have is not so much a church or religious revival, but a family revival!*

I think the Bible supports this idea. Malachi 4:6 talks about fathers turning their hearts to their children as a fundamental way of saving the land from a curse. Although the exact nature of that curse is not explained in the text, most Americans would agree that teen suicide, high divorce rates, and frequent substance abuse (to name but a few) represent a substantial curse to the American way of life. Such a curse could be, in part, the unfortunate result of four decades of social policies, anti-family radicals, and an ignoring of moral wisdom that once freely flowed from our homes. The curse is literally *tearing our families apart.*

The beginning of national revival, then, begins when elected officials, educators, lawyers, media representatives, and church leaders finally acknowledge that the family has been and is the most stabilizing and cohesive unit in the history of global civilization. As I have stated above, families in bondage need freedom from bureaucratic red tape. In line with my thinking is a report by the Family Research Council in Washington, DC that provides its readers with an analysis of social change affecting the family from 1950-1990 entitled "The American Family Under Siege." It concludes that documenting the problem is often one of the first steps to finding solutions:

> During the 1960s and 1970s America made a major economic commitment to the well being of its families and children. By 1976, there were more than 260 programs administered by twenty different agencies of the federal government whose primary mission was to benefit children. These programs responded to every imaginable problem. Each year hundreds of millions of dollars of new money is poured into them all in the name of helping the family.

> Yet during this same period of time, family life in America has, by any measurement, deteriorated. The family has lost too much of its authority to courts and rule-writers, too much of its voice in education and social policy, and too much of its resources to public officials at all levels. We have certainly made economic progress during recent years in turning back resources to the men and women who earn them through labor, invention, and investment. Now we face the unfinished agenda: Returning to households the autonomy that once was theirs, in a society stable and secure, where the family can generate and nurture what no government can ever produce—Americans who will responsibly exercise their freedom and, if

[12] *The American Family Under Siege* (Washington, DC: Family Research Council, 1989), 24.

necessary, defend it.[12]

What I like about this report is the emphasis on what the family can do that no substitute—whether it be government or even the church—has ever been able to do. I like the acknowledgment that, quite possibly, families, if left alone or not competed with, can and do thrive. Families have inherent in their environments a source of nurture that God put in them for the passing on of life skills and human development. Such an environment is a sacred domain that should be protected by law and enhanced by the church.

Nobody, and I mean nobody, should be allowed to take away the family's autonomy and strip it of its authority and its parental influence on children. Except in the rarest of cases, such as parental neglect or abuse, the family should be given license to be self-governing. It should continue in its protected place in American law and should not experience legislation that would lead to a "liberation by the state" of the child from, what Harvard legal scholar Lawrence Tribe calls, "the shackles of... family."[13]

Such a comment from a respected member of the legal community would appear to suggest that families are an intolerable burden to children; that children are the best judges of their own interests; and that, as such, they should be freed from all parental influences. Obviously Dorothy wouldn't agree. Certainly not after her experience over the

[13] Lawrance Tribe, *American Constitutional Law* (1092-94, 1978), 988.

rainbow. She would remind Mr. Tribe that families do a lot for children, like the time her Auntie Em nursed her back to health when she had a bad bout with the measles. Our nation and our churches need to realize more fully the family's enormous potential for healing, especially from the emotional and physical problems even modern medicine has not been able to deal with effectively. Ask any American and they will tell you that the most consistently effective cure for the common cold is Mom's chicken soup. Take out Mom and what do you get? Nothing but fowl!

As we look back in history we see that the quality of family life is very important to the strength of nations. There is a pattern in the rise and fall of great societies such as ancient Rome, Greece, and Egypt. When these societies were at the peak of their own power and prosperity, the family unit was strong and highly valued. When family life became weak in these societies, when the family was no longer valued—when goals became extremely individualistic—the societies began to deteriorate and eventually collapsed.[14]

What an ample warning to those who go searching for too much personal autonomy against the real rights and responsibilities of our homes. A fiercely independent spirit can lead one smack-dab into an ambush—remember the encounter of Dorothy with the Winged Monkeys—that may end up isolating us from family and friends and carrying us away captive to the castle of the Wicked Witch.

[14] Nick Stinnett, "Strong Families: A Portrait," *Prevention in Family Services* (Beverly Hills, CA: Sage Publications, 1983), 27.

"I'd turn back if I were you!" was an appropriate sign hung on a tree branch in the Haunted Forest. Today it should sound an alarm: spooks do exist who, like anarchistic libertarians, enjoy those who are caught up in the self-fulfilling and unrestrained pursuit of personal freedom. Like the spirits examined above, they delight in the false notion that we can run away from the perceived "shackles of family" and be assured of personal security and support.

It is only after we discover a bondage more threatening than our families had ever been that we cry out to them—like Dorothy did from her imprisonment in the castle of the Wicked Witch. Only then do we realize that isolation is its own hell and a despair far worse than family duty and commitment ever produced. Family becomes the one thing we long for when trouble strikes. "Like a bridge over troubled waters", it may be our only means of escape.

PART THREE

The Values of
Home and Family:
What We Need

Placing our faith in the families God has given us means discovering very specifically what values they offer us. If some families are in trouble, we need to discover those values that will get them out of trouble. We must discover what we need.

Part Three examines these values of home and family in some detail. Chapter 6 looks at strong families. Chapter 7 looks at the joys that come from very basic values. Chapter 8 looks at the specific values Dorothy brought home with her from Oz. Chapter 9 discovers what it means to find a home in God by examining the shift in values and priorities that happens to people who confront death and loss.

Six

Strong Families

When Dorothy and her three friends entered the Emerald City, one of the first things they noticed was a horse that changed color, from purple to blue, then green, then red. When they asked what kind of horse that was, the coachman replied, "Why, that's the horse you've heard tell about. That's a horse of a different color."

Obviously such color-changing horses are rare, even in the land of Oz. But they do exist, perhaps more in number than Dorothy had ever realized. It's kind of like buying a new, shiny red automobile. Once we buy it and drive it off the lot, all we see is red cars everywhere we go! Well, you know why. It's just that we're more aware of red cars, having bought one ourselves. That's also true of strong families. We might think them to be quite rare, but encounter just one and, before we know it, we'll encounter another, and then another, and then another. It's just that we haven't been trained, like those in the Emerald City, to see the truly spectacular and wonderful things that are all around us in this land.

Yes, strong families do exist; it's just that we haven't developed the eyes to see them!

"We have many strong families throughout this nation and the world," says Dr. Nick Stinnett, a pioneer in family strengths research, and a close, personal friend. The problem is, he contends, that there has been so little written about them. "On the newsstands we see many books and magazine articles about what's wrong with families.... Certainly we need information about positive family models and what strong families are like."[1]

It was with this in mind that Dr. Stinnett and others launched the Family Strengths Research Project, a search that has taken him throughout our nation as well as to other parts of the world.

"Our search began in Oklahoma.... More recently we have completed a national study of strong families representing all regions of the nation, an investigation of strong Russian

[1] Nick Stinnett, "Strong Families: A Portrait," *Prevention in Family Services* (Beverly Hills, CA: Sage Publications, 1983), 28.

immigrant families, a study of black families, and an examination of strong families from various countries in South America." And the search continues.

Today Dr. Stinnett and I have completed a statewide research project dealing with "the secrets of strong adolescents" that has already gone national. In this research project we had the assistance of the Cooperative Extension Service of Texas A & M University to help identify teens perceived to be doing well. We asked the Home Economics Extension Agent in each of the counties of Texas to recommend young men and women that the agent considered particularly strong. The results have been exciting and have been presented in our book, *Good Kids* published by Doubleday in 1996. It affirms loudly and clearly that strong adolescents from strong homes *do* exist and have some valuable insights to share with those wanting to build family or adolescent strengths.

THE SIX QUALITIES OF STRONG FAMILIES

The questions asked of families in these studies covered a broad range of concerns. For example, Dr. Stinnett asked how they dealt with conflict, communication patterns, and power structure. "When we analyzed the vast quantity of information," Stinnett writes, "we found six qualities that stood out among these strong families." [2] These qualities, he

[2] Stinnett, 30.

explains, seemed pivotal for both strength and happiness, and were found to characterize strong families in all of the research studies he has conducted.

What are family strengths?

According to Stinnett, they "are those relationship patterns, interpersonal skills and competencies, and social and psychological characteristics which create a sense of positive family identity, promote satisfying and fulfilling inter-action among family members, encourage the development of the potential of the family group and individual family members, and contribute to the family's ability to deal effec-tively with stress and crises."[3]

Summarized below is a brief synopsis of each char-acteristic:

1 *Commitment*—This strength is a commitment to the family. It is a promise of time and energy. Commitment in strong families means that the family as a whole is committed to seeing that each member reaches his or her potential. It does not mean that the individuals suffer so that the family can grow.

2 *Communication*—Effective communication in strong families involves clear, direct channels between the speaker and the listener. Families develop compli-cated ways of communicating. In fact, members may be unaware just what they are "saying" by a certain

[3] Nick Stinnett, "Strengthening Families," *Family Perspective* 13 (1979) 3-5

word, phrase or action. Individuals use a combination of verbal and nonverbal actions to get their messages across to others. Strong families have learned to communicate directly and to use consistent verbal and nonverbal behaviors.

3   Appreciation—The showing of appreciation is a result of the interworkings of commitment, wellness, communication and the other family strengths as well. It involves being able to recognize the beautiful, positive aspects of others and to let them know that you value these qualities. It also means being able to receive compliments yourself.

4   Time together—Spending time together as a family can be the most rewarding experience for humans. Two important features of time together are quality and quantity. Strong families spend meaningful time with each other and they do it a lot. This gives a family an identity that can be had in no other way.

5   High degree of religious orientation—These strong families went to church together often and they participated in religious activities together.... There are indications that this religious quality went deeper than going to church or participating in religious activities together. It could most appropriately be called a commitment

---

[4] Traits 1, 2, 3, 4 and 6 are from Building Family Strengths: A Manual for Families (Lincoln, NE: University of Nebraska Press, 1986), 8-9; Trait 5 is from Stinnett, "Strong Families: A Portrait," 34-35.

[5] Stinnett, "Strong Families: A Portrait," 35.

to a spiritual lifestyle. Words are inadequate to communicate this, but what many of these families said was that they had an awareness of God or a higher power that gave them a sense of purpose and gave their family a sense of support and strength. The awareness of this higher power in their lives helped them to be more patient with each another, more forgiving, quicker to get over anger, more positive, and more supportive in their relationships.

6   *The ability to deal with stress, conflict, and crises*—All of the previous strengths combine to make an inner core of power for families. This core serves as a resource for those times when conflicts and crises come. It helps reduce stress and prevent many conflicts and crises. Strong families are able to survive and even grow in hard times.[4]

LOOKING AT THE POSITIVE

The qualities that characterized the strong families in the above research coincide with what other researchers have reported who examined healthy families "It is interesting," writes Stinnett "that most of these qualities that we found to characterize strong families have been found to be lacking in families that are having severe relationship problems and in

---

[4] Traits 1, 2, 3, 4 and 6 are from *Building Family Strengths: A Manual for Families* (Lincoln, NE: University of Nebraska Press, 1986), 8-9; Trait 5 is from Stinnett, "Strong Families: A Portrait," 34-35.

families broken by divorce."[5] It would appear that this fact supports the validity of Stinnett's research and calls for the importance of these six qualities in building family strengths in our families. But "in order to build stronger families in the future we must match our remedial services [crisis-counseling, for example] with preventive services [education and enrichment]."[6] Stinnett concludes:

> We must turn from our preoccupation with pathology and the commonly accepted practice of spending all our energies doing "patchwork" and "picking up the wrecks." This approach is more expensive—both financially and in terms of human suffering. In order to be most effective we must make preventive services and programs available early in the lives of individuals and families to provide them with skills, knowledge, motivation, and positive models that can help build family strengths.... Strong families are the roots of our well-being as individuals and as a society. The dream of facilitating strong families that produce emotionally and socially healthy individuals can be realized. The positive potential for the family is great.[7]

The discussion above is my attempt to highlight the importance of families. It is also my attempt to get you to see that you probably have strengths and have never stopped to

[5] Stinnett, "Strong Families: A Portrait," 35.

[6] Stinnett, "Strong Families: A Portrait," 37.

[7] Stinnett, 38.

think about them before. And that's okay. Until Nick Stinnett and others pointed them out to me, I never noticed them either. All I could see was the negative. In a way, that's all I was ever trained to see. With all the bad things being said about families these days, is it any wonder that we believe the only thing to do is run away and stay away?

Dorothy had to have them pointed out to her, too! Remember her brief visit with Professor Marvel? To convince her to go home, he helped her recall all the good things her Auntie Em had done. With tears in her eyes she jumped up, grabbed her things, and said, "Why, I've got to get home." It was an "ah-ha!" experience. The light went on. She realized what she was doing: she was running away from the only people who had ever really loved her, nurtured her, and protected her from a cruel and unforgiving world.

In my mind, I'd like to think that since Toto shows up in the last remaining moments of the film that maybe—just maybe—Auntie Em and Uncle Henry finally understand. I like to believe they finally stand up to ol' Miss Gulch. Looking her straight in the eye they say, "Begone, before we drop our house on you!"

They act together and rally around Dorothy like any strong family would. Yes! United we stand, divided we fall. That's the message. So go home. Learn to forgive and forget—God will show you how. Then learn to stay home with the help of some good friends. Tell your family that you love them, before it's too late. And for heaven's sake, please show others the way home too. If need be, take an ax and some courageous, loving, and wise friends and break down that chamber door in the Wicked Witch's castle. Then run as fast as you can in the opposite direction and never look back. Stay steady on course on that yellow brick road, and tell each other with a sigh: There's no place like home."

Seven

The Joys of
Basic Values

Only author Max Lucado could have so poignantly
captured in print the desire to go home:

> I'm almost home. After five days, four hotel beds, eleven restau-
> rants, and twenty-two cups of coffee, I'm almost home. After
> eight airplane seats, five airports, two delays, one book, and five
> hundred and thirteen packages of peanuts, I'm almost home.

The plane resonates under me. A baby cries behind me. Businessmen converse around me. Cool air blows from a hole above me. But all that matters is what is before me—home.

Home. It was my first thought when I awoke this morning. It was my first thought when I stepped down from the last podium. It was my first thought when I said good-bye to my last host at the last airport. There's no door like the one to your own house. There's no better place to put your feet than under your own table. There's no coffee like coffee out of our own mug. There's no meal like the one at your own table. And there's no embrace like the one from your own family.

Home. The longest part of going home is the last part—the plane's taxiing to the terminal from the runway. I'm the fellow the flight attendant always has to tell to sit down. I'm the guy with one hand on my briefcase and the other on my seat belt. I have learned that there is a critical split second in which I can bolt down the aisle into the first-class section before the tributaries of people begin emptying into the main aisle.

I don't do that on every flight.... only when I'm going home. There is a leap of the heart as I exit the plane. I almost get nervous as I walk up the ramp. I step past people. I grip my satchel. My stomach tightens. My palms sweat. I walk into the lobby like an actor walking onto a stage. The curtain is lifted, and the audience stands in a half-moon. Most of the people see that I'm not the one they want and look past me. But from the side I hear the familiar shriek of two little girls. "Daddy!" I turn and see them—faces scrubbed, standing on chairs, bouncing up and down in joy as the man in their life walks toward them. Jenna stops bouncing just long enough to clap. She applauds! I don't know who told her to do that, but you can bet I'm not going to tell her to stop.

Behind them I see a third face—little Sara, only a few months old. Deeply asleep, she furrows her brow slightly in reaction to the squealing. And then I see a fourth face—my wife's face. Somehow, she has found time to comb her hair, put on a new dress, put on that extra sparkle. Somehow, though wrung out and done in, she will make me feel that my week is the only week worth talking about.

Faces of home.

That is what makes the promise at the end of the Beatitudes so compelling: "Rejoice and be glad, because great is your reward in heaven."

What is our reward? Home.[1]

Lucado has also drawn an important parallel between our journey home and being heaven bound—our final

[1] Max Lucado, *The Applause of Heaven* (Dallas: Word Publishing, 1990), 181-183.

journey. It's because of our reward—our heavenly home—
that life here on earth ought to be affected. We ought to live
differently because we believe we are going to a far better
place than we have ever known, a place far better than the
imaginations and fantasies of a little girl from Kansas who
longs to be over the rainbow. It's a place where troubles *do*
melt like lemon drops and where clouds *will* be far behind us.

SAYING GOOD-BYE TO HAVING IT ALL

But how ought we to live differently while we're here?
What do we have to give up? What ought we to embrace? I
suggest that we need to say good-bye to the dream of having
it all that our culture holds out to us. We need to rediscover
the simpler joys of life at home and the basic values of things
that last.

The same media that so often chronicles the desires of
Americans once dubbed the 1990s the "We decade." With a
renewed focus away from trendiness and materialism, *Time*
magazine reported that Americans are searching for "a
simpler life with deeper meaning."[2]

These are the humble makings of a revolution in progress:
macaroni and cheese. Timex watches. Volunteer work.
Insulated underwear. Savings accounts. Local activism. Sleds.
Pajamas. Sentimental movies. Primary colors. Mixed-breed
dogs. Bicycles. Cloth diapers. Shopping at Wal-Mart. Small-

[2] "The Simple Life," *Time* (April 8, 1991), 58.

town ways. Iceberg lettuce. Family reunions. Board games. Hang-it-yourself wallpaper. Push-it-yourself lawn mowers. Silly Putty.

See the pattern? It's as genuine as Grandma's quilt. After a ten-year bender of gaudy dreams and goddess commercialism, Americans are starting to trade down. They want to reduce their attachments to status symbols, fast track careers, and great expectations of Having It All. Upscale is out; downscale is in. Yuppies are an ancient civilization. Flaunting money is considered gauche: if you've got it, please keep it to yourself— or give some away!

In place of materialism, many Americans are embracing simpler pleasures and homier values. They've been thinking hard about what really matters in their lives, and they've decided to make some changes. What matters is having time for family and friends, rest and recreation, good deeds and spirituality.[3]

In a *Time*/CNN poll of 500 adults, 89 percent said it was more important to spend time *with family!*[4] This major shift in "America's private agenda" probably goes back as far as the stock-market crash of 1987, speculates *Time* reporter Janice Castro. Others "were awakened by individual experience: the plight of a homeless neighbor,

[3] Ibid.
[4] Ibid.

the collapse of a bank, a friend's job loss."[5] And, I might add, the death of a loved one has given "many people an uneasy feeling about the Roaring Eighties."[6] To sum it all up, consider Janice Castro's clever "Now and Then" mini-biographies:

THEN	NOW
The former apparel-industry executive used to travel on business almost every day. Home was where she replaced her suitcase.	Karen Glance jumped the fast track to operate a food market in her St. Paul neighborhood. "I'm tired at night, but it's a healthy tired."
Until last year, Barry Blake, then a liquor-industry executive, was living lavishly in a Manhattan penthouse and scrambling up the career ladder.	Blake runs an apple winery and cider mill in Vermont. "The old corporate chase doesn't mean anything to me anymore."
He built the largest stock mutual fund in the country, worth $13 billion. But he had no time to spend with his children. At 46, he quit.	Instead of picking stocks from dawn to dusk, Peter Lynch gets up early to make peanut-butter sandwiches for his three daughters.
A graduate of Harvard Law, he had his pick of major firms. When he turned his back on them, he recalls, "my parents were appalled."	Joe Holland hung out his shingle in Harlem, where he founded a homeless shelter. He now operates a travel bureau and a restaurant.

[5] Ibid.
[6] Ibid.

Even the *Wall Street Journal* seems to be catching wind of this new shift in American priorities. An article entitled "Family Vs. Work" in its June 12, 1991 issue, explains how Tom Clancy, best-selling author of *The Hunt for Red October* and other novels, chose to decline a US Senate seat from Maryland in favor of spending more time with his five-year-old daughter, Katie. The article wisely concludes:

> As most parents know, life... presents some pretty tall obstacles to building strong families.... But as Barbara Bush told the Wellesley grads of 1990: "At the end of your
> life, you will not regret not having passed one more test, not winning one more verdict, or not closing one more deal. You will regret time not spent with a husband, a friend, a child, or a parent."

Judging from their recent actions, Tom Clancy, Peter Lynch, Joe Holland, Karen Glance, and Barry Blake would undoubtedly agree. Add to that list Michael O'Donnell, who eventually learned to practice what he preached thanks to the most unlikely of pedagogues—a dying daughter.

Precious Cara taught me more in *death* than I had learned in over forty years of *life*. She has ministered to my restless heart with the eternal gift of a heart now at rest in God.

Eight

A Kindly Philosophy:
Values Learned from Oz

No doubt you are familiar with Robert Fulghum's bestseller *All I Really Need to Know I Learned in Kindergarten*. This wonderful little book—so irksome to literary scholars and serious academic types—has found a home in the hearts of millions of Americans who agree with Fulghum that wisdom is not found at the top of the graduate-school mountain, but in the sand pile at Sunday school.

"Within simplicity lies the sublime"—so reads a *San Francisco Chronicle* review. And Fulgham's philosophical simplicity is indeed prominent prose that finds wonderment and meaning in those little experiences that usually go unnoticed and unappreciated.

Even Fulgham's creed provides much insight for the young at heart:

> I *believe that imagination is stronger*
> *than knowledge.*
> That *myth is more potent than history.*
> That *dreams are more powerful than facts.*
> That *hope always triumphs over experience.*
> That *laughter is the only cure for grief*
> And I *believe that love is stronger*
> *than death.*[1]

Just as Fulgham's book presents an ethical code we all once cherished—share everything, play fair, don't hit people, put things back where you found them, etc.—so, too, The *Wizard of* Oz has a message of enduring quality that conveys simply, clearly and powerfully the importance of maintaining values in one's life.

All throughout The *Wizard of* Oz, we are confronted with the best that once was America; so much so that "time has been powerless to put its kindly philosophy out of fashion" (inserted into the picture immediately after the opening

[1] Robert Fulghum, *All I Really Needed to Know I Learned in Kindergarten* (New York: Ballentine Books, 1988), author's preface.

credits in 1938). It is no wonder, then, why MGM dedicated the film to "the Young in Heart"—for it has been their loyalty to the film's timeless message that has made *The Wizard of Oz* the most widely-seen and most beloved motion picture of all time.

And so, in the tradition of Fulgham's book, these are the things I learned from watching *The Wizard of Oz*:

1 Be kind to things and people.

2 A stranger is a friend you haven't met yet.

3 When you find a need in your way, fill it.

4 Apologize when you do something wrong.

5 Stand up for what is right, regardless of the consequences.

6 Be loyal to your friends.

7 Good manners never hurt anyone.

8 There's no place like home.

BE KIND TO THINGS AND PEOPLE

More than any other word, I believe "kind" is an adjective that best describes *The Wizard of Oz*. It is a word that has lost significance in the moral, social, and behavioral conditions of modern American society. Yet there was a time in our nation's history when kindness was a virtue both modeled and taught.

One-room schoolhouses once displayed the word

no matter who they are, where they've come from, or how little they possess.

Yes, kindness is love. And the world will know we are Christians by its abundance in our lives.

A STRANGER IS A FRIEND YOU HAVEN'T MET YET

Dorothy's ability to make friends is quite extraordinary by today's standards. She has a gift for intimacy that brings three isolated and lonely beings to an emotional banquet of caring gestures and words of affection. Who can forget the Lion, Tin Man, and Scarecrow bidding farewell to Dorothy? Obviously, they wouldn't have been hurting so much if they hadn't learned to care so much—all thanks to Dorothy.

It should not surprise us that friendliness is another Scouting principle to be committed to memory and explained in a Scout's own words. I can even remember when some report cards included friendliness as a category to be evaluated with the words "satisfactory", or "unsatis-factory", at the discretion of an elementary school teacher

The ability to make friends was once considered a good childhood predictor of later social adaptability and grace. We not only taught it in our homes but encouraged it in our schools. To make friends was a sign of wellness that spoke of an essential characteristic called "trust."

We once had faith in our fellow man. But this is no longer true. Today suspicion and cynicism are hallmarks of maturity.

"kindness" on bulletin boards.

The Boy Scout Handbook taught that a scout was, among other things, kind. The concept was one of the twelve points of the Scout Law that was to be a foundation on which the whole Scouting movement was built.

Kindness is so important a concept that the Bible records it second only to patience in a list of the chief characteristics of love (see 1 Cor. 13:4).

Dorothy has kindness in abundance. When the Cowardly Lion attacks Toto, for instance, Dorothy is appalled at the Lion's apparent lack of virtue: "Why, don't you know that you're not supposed to pick on things weaker than you are?" she asks with a sense of childlike surprise. Her response comes straight out of the *Scout Handbook*: "He is a friend to animals... [and] will not hurt any living creature... but will strive to save and protect all harmless life."

We would all like to be kind as Dorothy was to things weaker than she was. Her love for Toto reflected that same kindness that "strives to save and protect." Referring to Toto's mishap with Miss Gulch, she asked the raggedy mutt, "Did she hurt you?" Whisking him off to safety, Dorothy believed her family would be equally indignant at Miss Gulch's unkindly behavior.

To be kind is to be content with the weak. It is to tolerate harmless life, even when it appears to have very little redeeming value. It is a feeling of being connected to all who walk this world, believing that they have a right to kindness

Strangers are to be feared. Many of us do not even know who our neighbors are and have spent so little time cultivating new relationships that we have to travel hundreds of miles just to visit one friend.

Not so with Dorothy. Everywhere she went she made friends. Even the Wicked Witch's own guards would eventually come to love this little girl from Kansas and her irrefutable hope and good will. She simply brought out the best in people by holding their hands and skipping down a yellow brick road as they sang a song of great expectations together. Such behavior engenders hope:

> Hope looks for the good in people instead of harping on the worst in them.
> Hope opens doors where despair closes them.
> Hope discovers what can be done instead of grumbling about what cannot be done.
> Hope draws its power from a deep trust in God and the basic goodness of mankind.
> Hope lights a candle instead of cursing the darkness. Hope regards problems, small or large, as opportunities.
> Hope cherishes no illusions, nor does it yield to cynicism.
>
> —SOURCE UNKNOWN

WHEN YOU FIND A NEED IN YOUR WAY, FILL IT

When traveling the yellow brick road, Dorothy was faced

with a number of early challenges. First was a scarecrow stuck on a pole in a cornfield. Second was a tin woodsman who had rusted into place. Last was a lion who hadn't slept in weeks. So what does she do?

She stops. She finds out what's wrong. Then she tries to help out the best she can. She is the definitive "Good Samaritan."

Dorothy was the kind of person who had been taught to look out for her fellow man... to be prepared for service. No doubt her motto was like the old Scout slogan: "Do a Good Turn Daily."

Dorothy was a "do-gooder"—in the best possible sense. In her life on the farm she had perhaps heard the stories of World War I veterans who had risked their own lives saving others overseas. "Someday," she was told, "even you may join the roster of small town heroes—if you are prepared!" Dorothy was prepared to do good, sometimes fearlessly.

Perhaps it's what we admire most about her. She is a courageous little role model for kids who need a hero their own age.

She reminds me of that little boy who brings Jesus five small barley loaves and two small fish to feed five thousand hungry people (see John 6:1-13). It takes a lot of guts to walk up to an adult and offer help, especially in a day and age when children were to be seen and not heard.

But that's what this small boy did. And no one went away hungry that day, I can tell you!

One of Dorothy's outstanding character traits was noticing the needy.

How many others had traveled that same yellow brick road before Dorothy? Did they stop? Did they listen? Did they offer to help? Apparently not. No one but that little girl ever noticed. And noticing the plight of others, according to the Bible, is a very big deal.

A rich man was also bad at noticing people, especially people in need (see Luke 16:19-31). Jesus tells us that this rich man walked by Lazarus—a poor, starving man covered with ulcerated sores—every day, and never noticed him. We are told by Jesus that after Lazarus died, he was "carried by the angels to the bosom of Abraham"; but when the rich man died he went to a place of indescribable torture.

At this point, Barclay—in his commentary on Luke—asks an interesting question: what was the sin of the rich man that sent him to hell? What follows is Barclay's chilling response:

The sin of [the rich man] was that he never noticed Lazarus, that he accepted him as part of the landscape and simply thought it perfectly natural and inevitable that Lazarus should lie in pain and hunger while he wallowed in luxury.

The sin of [the rich man] was that he could look on the world's suffering and need and feel no answering sword of grief and pity pierce his heart; he looked at a fellowman, hungry and in pain, and did nothing about it. His was the punishment of the man who never noticed.

It is a terrible warning that the sin of [the rich man] was not that he did wrong things, but that he did nothing?[2]

We see what we want to see. In fact, we see what our eyes have been trained to see. And Dorothy's upbringing had provided her with the most wonderful eyes to see—to notice even "the least of these."

Then the King will say to those on his right, "Come, you who are blessed by my father; take your inheritance, the kingdom prepared for you since the creation of the world. For I was hungry and you gave me something to eat, I was thirsty and you gave me something to drink, I was a stranger and you invited me in, I needed clothes and you clothed me, I was sick and you looked after me, I was in prison and you came to visit me."

Then the righteous will answer him, "Lord, when did we see you hungry and feed you, or thirsty and give you something to drink? When did we see you a stranger and invite you in, or needing clothes and clothe you? When did we see you sick or in prison and go to visit you?"

The King will reply, "I tell you the truth, whatever you did for one of the least of these brothers of mine, you did for me"

[2] William Barclay, *The Gospel of Luke: The Daily Bible Series* (Philadelphia: Westminister Press, 1975), 214.

(Matt. 25:34-40).

APOLOGIZE WHEN YOU DO SOMETHING WRONG

When Glenda asks Dorothy whether she is a good witch or bad witch, she responds, "I'm not a witch at all. Why, witches are old and ugly." Immediately the Munchkins burst into polite laughter.

"Why are they laughing?" asks Dorothy.

Because," says Glenda, "I am a witch."

"Oh, I beg your pardon," Dorothy says while curtsying, "But I've never heard of a beautiful witch before."

While it is not to be argued here the biblical fact that all witches—whether considered "good" or "bad"—are evil in the sight of God, it's the response of Dorothy that is noteworthy. As soon as she is aware of possibly having been offensive, she apologizes. Her curtsy is further evidence of a well-bred little girl who respectfully acknowledges her inappropriate remark.

Ah, those were the days! Remember when we were taught not only to respect our elders, but to own up to our mistakes? I can even remember when, as a young lieutenant in the United States Army Reserve, I was trained to say, "No excuse, Sir" as the only legitimate response for having done something wrong or for not having completed an assignment on time.

"Old fashioned," you say. Maybe so. But I believe we have

a moral crisis in our country that centers around an inability on the part of the vast majority of Americans to admit when they're wrong.

Parents blame schools when children misbehave. Teachers fear losing their jobs when accusing a student of wrongdoing, especially when the professional integrity of the teacher who made the charge in the first place is disputed by the pupil. Store clerks handle the complaints of patrons with scorn and contempt. Even political figures refuse to shoulder any fault, repeatedly blaming everyone else when things go awry. This is not good!

Whatever happened to parents who brought their children back to school to apologize to a teacher or classmate, even after amends had been made? Positive reinforcement, right? Or how about the punishment at home that followed being punished at school? Store clerks were once taught "the customer is always right" and were given instructions on how to handle grievances with apologetic skill and grace. Even President Truman made the phrase "the buck stops here" a popular hallmark of his administration.

To apologize is to demonstrate character. To admit when we're wrong and offer sincere regrets is a principal key that unlocks the door to lasting relationships—in our homes, churches, and communities. It is an ability we encourage in our leaders and have come to expect as protocol in our religious affairs. "Therefore," concludes Jesus, "if you are offering your gift at the altar and there remember that your brother has something against you, leave your gift there in front of the altar. First go and be reconciled to your brother; then come and offer your gift" (Matt. 5:23-24).

How satisfying it is to witness the gracious apology of Dorothy for having melted the Wicked Witch of the West. Though above reproach, she was never above humbling herself and acknowledging the possibility of being wrong.

Likewise, I believe such humility will ultimately affect us and provide a contentment of divine proportions. Why? Because the Bible tells us that if we admit our mistakes and moral failures, Jesus "is faithful and just and will forgive us our sins and purify us from all unrighteousness" (1 John 1:9).

STAND UP FOR WHAT IS RIGHT
REGARDLESS OF THE CONSEQUENCES

There's an interesting story in the Bible that records an important confrontation between two of the apostles, Paul and Peter.

Paul believed and taught that salvation offered by Jesus Christ was available to everyone. Even though a great many of the early converts to Christianity were Jewish, Paul did not teach that to become a Christian you had to first become a Jew. If he had, it would have meant potential Christians would be required by Jewish law to adopt many of the old customs and traditions of Judaism, not to mention being circumcised at the time of one's conversion.

Peter agreed with Paul but was later influenced by James.

James was adamant about being circumcised and formed a group that later became known as "Judaizers." This group that now claimed Peter as a member went to Christian communities established by Paul to get new converts to become Jews and to eventually succumb to the painful and often life-threatening ordeal of circumcision.

It is my belief that Paul's confrontation with Peter over this and other church-related issues as recorded in Galatians sustains the purity of Christ's gospel to this day. If Paul, whose apostleship was suspect, had not had the courage to stand up to Peter—the "super apostle"—regardless of the consequences, Christianity might still require converts to become Jews first. Males might be required to be circumcised as the only legitimate response to the "good news" of Jesus Christ.

To stand up for what is right, regardless of the consequences, is no easy task. As hard as it is to imagine, Paul could have lost his life if Peter and his followers had overreacted and done violence to him for challenging the integrity of Peter's apostleship. History records, however, that Peter fell under deep conviction and was persuaded by Paul to seek the forgiveness of the entire Christian community. Although Dorothy's confrontation with the Wizard of Oz is less spectacular, it is nevertheless a pivotal point in the story. If Dorothy had not had the courage to stand up to the Wizard of Oz for not keeping his promises, then quite possibly the Lion would never have gotten his courage, the Tin Man would never have gotten his heart, and the Scarecrow would never have gotten his brains. Even Dorothy and Toto might never have found their way back over the rainbow. This is a valuable lesson. We need children who know how to stand up for what is right and say no to drugs, alcohol, sexual promiscuity, and temptation—who choose not to "conform any longer to the pattern of this world" (Rom. 12:2a).

In the training of our children, there must be a commitment to certain uncompromising truths. These values must be reflected in the choices they make.

Children need to know that even if we or some other adult—even an "angel from heaven" Paul would argue—should try to get them to do that which is contrary to the Word of God, they should stand up for their convictions and "approve what God's will is—his good, pleasing, and perfect will" (Rom. 12:2b).

BE LOYAL TO YOUR FRIENDS

The Bible tells a story of incredible loyalty among warriors—a loyalty so strong that it caused men to risk their lives and go up against overwhelming odds for the sake of providing even the simplest of requests for a friend. The story is about King David and "his mighty men." The story is extraordinary.

As David looks upon the strong men who had come to him in exile—many of them even related to David's current nemesis, King Saul—he smiles. Uriah notices and has to smile himself.

I would die for this man, my king, Uriah thinks. *Here we are, forced away from friends and family, a small band compared to King Saul's vast armies. Yet God's might is here. God is among us.*

To David's amazement, men continue to pour into his camp by the hundreds and thousands, preparing the way for him to become king of Israel. Still, he draws his true strength from God and from a small band of warriors who gathered round him in his early days of exile.

Hidden away in the mountains, the mighty men in that first, small group of fugitives had been forced to depend on each other. As they prepared to do God's work in the land, the Lord changed the brawny, violent men. They hunted to help feed others. They fought as a team. They were willing to die for each other. The warrior's might remained, but their loyalty was directed toward David and his God.

Uriah studies David as the leader watches his men hone their battle skills. His heart once again swells with pride and a powerful brotherly love as he recalls a recent feat accomplished by three of his fellow chiefs. David had been in the stronghold when the three had come to watch the Philistine garrison at Bethlehem. Their leader longed for water, and wished aloud, "Oh, that someone would get me a drink of water from the well near the gate of Bethlehem."

David was giving no command. He was issuing no order. He was simply thinking aloud. But David's warriors—his closest friends—rushed from the stronghold, broke through the Philistine lines, and drew water from the well near the gate of Bethlehem.

Fighting their way back through fierce Philistine war-mongers, the three men arrived once again at David's cave. Breathless and bleeding, they proudly handed David the cup of water. He looked at the clear, cool liquid. He looked at his men, moved beyond words.

The king could not drink the water. Instead he poured it out before the Lord.

"God forbid that I should do this!" he said. "Should I drink the blood of these men who went at the risk of their lives?" Such was the incredible love, the extravagant devotion of these heroic men to their leader.... Their military might did not come from their brawn alone. God's power emanated from their hearts—hearts that were loyal... even to the point of death.[3]

This story, as recorded in 1 Chronicles 11:15-19, is certainly more significant than a fantasy adventure like *The Wizard of Oz*. Yet a number of the principles demonstrated above are also found among Dorothy and her "mighty men."

I love the part in the movie when the Scarecrow, the Tin

Man, and the Lion risk their own lives to rescue Dorothy from the castle of the Wicked Witch. Or when the Scarecrow pulls Dorothy from the grasp of some hostile, talking trees. Especially delightful is the loyalty of the three when, after getting their gifts from the Wizard's black bag, they band together and shout, "Hey, what about Dorothy?"

Loyalty is a theme found throughout *The Wizard of Oz*. Loyalty between friends. Loyalty to the goal of getting to the Emerald City. Loyalty to a little dog named Toto. Even Toto proves to be loyal when, escaping from the Witch's castle, he runs to the Scarecrow, Tin Man, and Lion to bring them to Dorothy's aid.

Yes, this is the kind of loyalty we reward with the words, "I knew you'd come," even when no one else does. This is the loyalty we see among Dorothy and her mighty men—where "true blue" becomes a hallmark of their friendship and faithfulness their undying creed.

GOOD MANNERS NEVER HURT ANYONE

Once a student addressed me as "Mikey." Although he probably did not intend for me to take him seriously, I quickly corrected him and told him that I preferred to be addressed as "Michael" or "Dr. O'Donnell." "Mikey" was just more than I could bear.

The incident left me to ponder why it is that young adults, when addressing older adults, are not more courteous. Why

do they not use the time-honored titles of a previous generation, such as "Sir" and "Ma'am" or even "Mr." "Mrs.," "Miss,"
or, if you prefer, "Ms."?

Maybe this attitude comes from my military background
or some other reactionary flaw. It could simply be that I
looked forward to one day receiving some of the same
courtesy as an adult that I had extended as a child to my
elders and to those who were in authority. Whatever the case,
manners never hurt anyone—that's what I was taught.
Maybe—just maybe—manners helped me become the kind of
citizen that defined the men of my father's generation.

To be a gentleman was once a highly-touted trait. You
were expected to open doors for ladies, tip your hat to
women passing by, rise from your chair when a guest entered
the room, and offer your seat on a crowded bus. Although
this was taught to me by my dad, it was reinforced in the
public school and expected of me as one of the ideals of the
Boy Scout Law.

I can even remember being told by my Scout leader—
who, incidentally, I was expected to greet with a salute—of an
old man who went to see one of the Olympic games in
ancient Greece. Because he had arrived late, there wasn't a
single seat left. A Spartan youth noticed the old man
standing while those nearby were comfortably seated. The
young man called for his elder to come near and gave him his
seat. Suddenly, the coliseum erupted into wild applause as a

[1] Michael A. O'Donnell and Michelle Morris, *Heart of the Warrior* (Abilene, TX:
Abilene Christian University Press, 1993), 2-4.

group of young Athenians witnessed the event. At this, the old man turned toward them and said: "Indeed, you Athenians know the right thing to do—but, it takes a Spartan to do it!"

No doubt many in Oz knew the right things to do, but it took an unassuming little girl from Kansas to do it. Where Dorothy came from, the old rules of etiquette protected her and society as a whole.

How things have changed. According to Linda Lichter of the *Wall Street Journal*, an America without chivalry may be embracing "a culture of anarchy" and "encouraging immediate gratification and maximum self-expression, whatever the cost." She continues:

> The men who lived by |chivalry| would be apalled to learn that today the fair sex is routinely verbally assaulted and that even obviously pregnant women are denied seats on trains. They would wonder how we could fight to put a few women on the Supreme Court and in corporate towers while stripping all women of the freedom to walk our streets in safety. This erosion of civility is due in part to feminists who saw chivalry as tyranny dressed in kid gloves. But that's not the only reason. Since the 1960s, an entire generation has gleefully rejected Victorian manners as rigid and snooty. Worse, manners were seen to perpetuate that great Puritan bugaboo—self-restraint. It was not always so. During the Civil War, American Victorians were stunned by the horrible evidence that, as Charles Darwin

had lately pointed out, humans were not one step below the angels but a few steps above primordial sludge. People took comfort in a greatly expanded etiquette code, which proved they could rise above their roots. The code covered every action from debating delicate subjects to the proper folding of a calling card. And self-restraint, taught in homes, schools and churches, came to shield women and blunt the sharp edges of a Darwinian world.[4]

Such manners, concludes Lichter, were an addendum to the laws of our land that enabled it to protect itself against offenses even the law cannot touch. Maybe manners never hurt anyone, but a lack of manners does. And I'll take my hat off to that any day!

THERE'S NO PLACE LIKE HOME

In an interview for *Christianity Today*, former education secretary and drug czar William Bennett says America is suffering from "cultural breakdown" and must revive its passion for a national recovery of moral values. In talking about his new book, *The De-valuing of America: The Fight for Our Culture and Our Children*, Bennett further defends his position.

Crime is way up. Child abuse is way up. Illegitimacy is way up. More than sixty-five percent of black children in this country

[4] "What Ever Happened to Chivalry?" *Wall Street Journal* (April 21, 1993).

are born out of wedlock. Family dissolution is up. Perhaps even more important, there are more and more children in this country who never live in a real family. They don't know what a father is. This is probably the single most important number we looked at. It has a lot to do with generating some of the other numbers. What we see is social breakdown, which is caused in part by moral breakdown. I identified the moral education of the young as the single most important task we have—in all generations, but emphatically now![5]

In my former work with fathers at the Center for Fathering, I found William Bennett to be right on target when he stated that "the single most important number" they looked at had to do with fathers. I agree: "It has a lot to do with generating some of the other numbers."

If we're going to talk about measuring cultural decline, then we had better fix our sights on home. If William Bennett is right about a lack of virtue being more important than the US economy—and I believe he is—then we had better consider where the moral education of America's young should begin. Although, as the article states, Thomas Jefferson is right for his "time-honored belief" that "schools should be places that teach kids how to read, write, count, think—and develop religious standards and morals," one needs to ask the question: where did Jefferson first learn about God? I dare say not in a one-room school house, but

[5] Interview with William Bennett , *Christianity Today* (September 13, 1993).

from his mother and father—of course!

If we are simply going to put the responsibility for "raising up a child in the way he should go" to educational institutions, then I believe we have missed one of the most valuable lessons I learned from *The Wizard Of Oz*. And that is: *There's no place like home* for the development of life skills and faith development. Home, not school, is where it all starts! It begins with parents, although it may be reinforced by teachers.

Even *The Boy Scout Handbook* acknowledges the home as the strategic place where it all begins. Consider a sample of the Scout Laws which include a discussion of the would-be Scout's home as the principal laboratory where values are to be first learned and practiced:

A Scout Is Loyal

Loyalty starts at home. You show this loyalty best by turning yourself into the kind of boy your parents would like you to be, by making them realize that you appreciate what they do for you, and by speaking about your home in such a way that people understand that you love it. You show your loyalty also by helping your parents make it into a happy place for a happy family. The place where you live may not be the finest in the neighborhood—but it is your home, and no palace will ever take its place in your heart.

A Scout Is Helpful

Your regular home duties are not good turns—those are things that are expected of you.

A Scout Is Courteous

First of all, be courteous in your own home. There are people with the reputation of being polite in public who seem to forget their manners when at home. Don't be one of them. A "please" and a "thank you" are easily said, and little helpful things easily done, yet they make your father and your mother and the other members of the family feel that you really do appreciate what they do for you.

A Scout Is Kind

If you have a dog or other animal pet of your own you are probably already kind to it. You want it to love you and you know that this will happen only if you take good care of it. You have to understand when it needs food and water and shelter and special attention. If you live on a farm you know how well poultry and livestock respond to good care.

A Scout Is Obedient

Obedience begins with your father and mother. When they

request you to do a thing, do it immediately and cheerfully—
even if you happen to be in the middle of a game or an exciting
TV program. Soldiers do not enjoy going into battle. But they
obey orders. They know what is expected of them and do it.[6]

Paul's message to the Ephesians also acknowledges
something more important than the economic injustice of
their day and its impact on the human predicament. His
radical solution moves beyond what politics can do to what
God can do by producing a "new creation"—beginning with
our homes. Reflecting on Paul's greater vision, John R.W.
Stott writes:

Paul has been outlining the new standards which God expects
of his new society, the church, especially in terms of its unity
and purity. These two qualities are indispensable to a life which
is both worthy of the calling and fitting to the status of the
people of God. He moves on now to the new relationships in
which God's new people inevitably find themselves, and in so
doing he concentrates in the rest of his letter on two further
dimensions of Christian living.

The first concerns the practical, down-to-earth relationships of
the home. For the divine family ceases to be a credible concept
if it is not itself subdivided into human families which display
God's love. What is the point of peace in the church if there is

[6] *Boy Scout Handbook*, 41-46.

no peace in the home?

These two responsibilities (home... on the one hand, and spiritual combat on the other) are quite different from each other. Husband and wife, parents and children... are tangible human beings, while the "principalities and powers" arrayed against us are invisible, intangible demonic beings. Nevertheless, if our Christian faith is to be of any practical value, it must be able to cope with both situations. It must teach us how to behave Christianly at home... and it must enable us to fight against evil in such a way that we stand and do not fall. Thus harmony in the home and stability in the fight are the two final topics which the apostle handles.

Detailed, practical instruction on Christian family life.., seems to have been given by the apostles from the beginning. Examples occur in the letters of both Paul and Peter. There is an urgent need in our day for similar plain moral education. Too much so-called "holiness teaching" emphasizes a personal relationship to Jesus Christ without any attempt to indicate its consequences in terms of relationships with the people we live... with. In contrast to such holiness-in-a-vacuum, which magnifies experiences and minimizes ethics, the apostles spelled out Christian duty in the concrete situations of everyday life ....

Luther in his Catechism seems to have been the first person to refer to these lists as *Haustafeln*, meaning literally "house tables" but often translated "tables of household duties." In recent years scholars have compared them with similar precepts both in the Jewish *halakah* (their corpus of law and tradition) and in Gentile literature, especially of the Stoics. That Jews, Stoics and Christians should all have been concerned about moral behavior in the home should not surprise us.[7]

I've said it before and I'll say it again: "as the home goes, so goes the church" and "as the church goes, so goes our nation." This is the significance of the home in relationship to the other above-mentioned principles gleaned from *The Wizard of Oz.* The simple conclusion of the matter is: Dorothy brought values to Oz that reflected a time in our nation's history when children were to "obey [their] parents in the Lord" (Ephesians 6:1) and "honor [their] father and mother" (verse 2) "that it may be well with [them] and [they may] live long on the earth" (verse 3).

A return to these simple yet indispensable lessons is in order if we are to reverse the current trend of cultural disintegration. By reviving them we revive ourselves and the contentment they once provided in marriage and family relationships.

Putting into practice a code of action is to place a premium on human relationships. This is where our greatest contentment is found and where fulfillment for the restless heart is secured. When I value more highly other people so

[7] John R.W Stott, *God's New Society* (Downers Grove, IL: Inter-Varsity Press, 1979), 213-214.

as to sacrifice my agenda for theirs, I have put love first and have in effect put those relationships on holy ground... made them sacred.

It may sound all too simple. But the best things in life usually are. That's why we need to return to a childlike sense of wonder and appreciation for what is common. Regarding this principle, *The Wizard of Oz* is wonderfully concise yet comprehensive. No one can watch it without being lifted a bit higher and challenged to "do unto others as you would have them do unto you."

George MacDonald illustrates this childlike wonder in the following poem:

THE CHRISTMAS CHILD

"Little one, who straight has come
Down the heavenly stair,
Tell us all about your home,
And the father there."
"He is such a one as I,
Like as like can be,
Do his will, and by and by,
Home and him you'll see."[8]

—GEORGE MACDONALD

"There is a childhood into which we have to grow,"

[8] MacDonald: *Discovering the Character of God*, ed. Michael R. Phillips, (Minneapolis: Bethany House, 1989), 150.

concludes MacDonald, "just as there is a childhood we must leave behind. Most of us, as we are leaving the one, as yet have scarce an inkling of the other. One is a childishness from which but few of those who are counted wisest among men have freed themselves. The other is a childlikeness, which is the highest gain of humanity."[9]

[9] Ibid.

Nine

Death and Loss:
Discovering a Home in God

This discussion of discovering the God-given values of home and family would not be complete without considering death and loss as a radical means of discovering a home in God. Looking at death as our last great adventure and then at Dorothy as a "prodigal daughter" who is lost, then found, helps us to appreciate and prioritize the sacredness of home and family.

DEATH: THE LAST GREAT ADVENTURE IN LIFE

I have already shared with you my personal encounter with death when my wife and I lost our daughter, Cara. We learned many lessons.

Heaven is God's home. Biblical descriptions of it leave no doubt that heaven will be a wonderful place.

Affirming to me, however, are the descriptions of heaven by innocent children who see the spiritual realm more clearly in death than we do in life. Terminally ill boys and girls paint a portrait of heaven with remarkable words that make our final journey home more informed by these little theologians of the afterlife. They teach us to trust God's words about a place where we "cease from troubling; and there the weary be at rest" (Job 3:17); that "the small and the great are there; and the servant is free from his master" (Job 3:19); that "there shall be no night there" (Rev. 21:25); that God will "command his angels" to lift us up "in their hands" (Ps. 91:11-12); and that, indeed, in our heavenly father's home "are many rooms" (John 14:2).

In a fascinating new book entitled A Window to Heaven, Dr. Diane Komp relates her journey to a vibrant faith in God as she treated young cancer patients. "If I were to believe," she writes, "it would require the testimony of reliable witnesses ...."[1]

---

[1] Diane Komp, A Window to Heaven (Grand Rapids, MI: Zondervan Publishing House, 1992), inside jacket cover.

Her "reliable witnesses" appeared in the suffering lives of the children she treated: children like Anna who mustered enough energy to sit up in her hospital bed and say, "Mommy, can you see them (angels)? Do you hear their singing?" Or young Donny, a boy with Down's syndrome and leukemia, who entertained his doctors with a mythical feast shortly before he died. Parents, too, bore witness to a God who restores life even in the face of death: the pain of divorce healed at the death of a son; a grieving morn and dad of twins who died within three months of each other: "Soon, Jorden, you will go to see Jesus and Nathan in heaven."[2]

The remarkable nature of this book drives home my point that the inevitability of life after death—guided by these "littlest of God's giants"—should positively impact our lives and family relationships. Even the thought of losing a loved one or having come close ought to get us to change our priorities and capture the essence of what it means to have treasures in heaven.

I would like to believe that perhaps it was the near-fatal blow to Dorothy's head that pulled her family back together again. Seeing her lying unconscious and on the brink of death may have caused her family to rethink their lack of responsiveness and their lack of a listening ear.

None of them would ever again dare take for granted—at least, not any time soon—the ponderings of a little girl and

[2] Ibid.

her need to be heard. Through tragedy and pain, they would treasure her as she now treasured them.

Unfortunately, not all of us get a second chance. Our greatest lessons regarding the value of our family members may come only after they are gone permanently. For some, only the death of a son or daughter, mother or father, brother or sister can provide a key to the meaning of human existence and the indispensable role our families play.

I know this to be true.

Here are accounts of how two others have responded to and learned from death.

World-renowned authority and counselor on death Elisabeth Kubler-Ross tells the story of Mrs. M., seventy-one years old, whose life was filled with discontentment and a troubled heart.

> One of her recurring statements was "if I could only do my life over, and know what I know now, I would do it so differently!" When she enlarged upon this, it came through that her whole life appeared to her as having been mostly wasted. Her life had been filled with anxiety because of several failures in marriage, several job changes, and many moves. Now in the hospital, looking back at her life, she saw herself without roots, friends, or meaningful relationships, and her fears were magnified by the awareness of her limited life expectancy.[3]

---

[3] Elizabeth Kubler-Ross, *Death: The Final Stage of Growth* (Englewood Cliffs, NJ: Prentice Hall, i975), preface.

The other account is by a person I met many years ago. While a student at Pepperdine University, I was a guest in the home of world-renowned author and lecturer Dr. Paul Tournier. I asked him what his next adventure in life was. Without hesitating he said, "To die.... death is my next great adventure in life." This was hardly the response I expected.

Now, many years later, I've come to appreciate those words and the contentment they bring my heart.

Paul had a focus and a philosophy of life that enabled him to face death with courage. This was apparently true for his wife, Nelly, as well. Over the years, Paul and I would occasionally correspond with each other about his views regarding theology and psychology. In one letter written in 1979, I shared with him the grief I was experiencing with my father's near-fatal bout with cancer. (I feared my father would not survive the year.) Paul sent back a letter with a rare gem inside—a never-before published account of losing his wife, Nelly, that originally was a letter written in French and sent to family and friends. I immediately had it translated into English.

I share this letter that (unlike the account of Mrs. M. as recorded by Kubler-Ross) reflects the full, vibrant life of Nelly. Hers was a life of contentment and a fulfilled heart—all because she shared it with another in the pursuit of great faith in God.

Dear Friends,

I thank you with all my heart for the warm sympathy that you have expressed to me on the occasion of Nelly's death. In reading so many affectionate, touching messages, on my behalf, and so many expressions of gratitude to her, I thought that a formal card of thanks would not be sufficient. Many of those who wrote to me would like some details about the events which led to her death, and about the sentiments with which I received them with her.

We departed happily for Athens, responding to the call of two religious movements to which we were attached by the profound bonds of friendship and communion in the faith—for five years with the first, and more than twenty-five years with the second. The first is the "Adventure of Living Conference" of Waco, Texas, and the second is "The Christian Union of Intellectuals" of Athens. On the 21st, on the occasion of my second conference to the Americans about Jesus and Socrates, two great speakers, many of our Greek friends had joined us. Nelly was happy, welcoming them one by one.

It was that same evening that she had a coronary thrombosis. She was hospitalized in the Emergency Service of Cardiology, and was wonderfully taken care of. We were both pleased by the affection and prayers of our Greek friends. And during these weeks, the long hours spent with her in her small hospital room, open to other distractions, also filled that special intimacy which had united us for half a century.

Nelly, however, wanted me to give the two promised conferences to the open public in Athens. My associates had the consideration not to tell me that, little by little, her condition was worsening—rather that it was getting better thanks to their cares. Her desire was to leave the hospital and rejoin me at the hotel. She was authorized to leave the 20th of May, and we spent the last three days of her life without ever leaving each other, in the peace, the love, the prayer, and the faith, and during which time she often said to me, "I am happy." Certainly, she still hoped, as did I, that the day of her return to Geneva was approaching, but without too many illusions. One day, she said to me, "Maybe it would have been just as well that I died from my infarction." "But you are happy that they saved your life." "Yes, to see my children and grandchildren again." Then she added, "If I were dead, I would be in heaven, and I would meet your parents that I never knew." "Oh, well," I responded, "they would thank you for having been the wife that you have been for their son."

The 23rd of May, on the morning of Ascension Day, our thoughts went to Geneva, where our grandson Gilles was going to pronounce the confirmation of his baptism in the old cathedral where my father had preached long ago, and where we shared many marvelous memories. But we also spoke very calmly of the eventuality of a new infarction, and she told me, "If I have another one, I will surely die, but you take your vacation just as if I were with you." A few minutes later, this dreaded crisis came unexpectedly. It lasted several moments, and Nelly was perfectly aware of what was happening to her.

It was a peaceful death, in the middle of a missionary journey. It crowned a life in which she had enough heart to share in my missionary vocation, to sustain me modestly, to be my intimate confidante, first in the era of the evangelization of the "Groups of Oxford," then in the new orientation of my career, in my task of being a writer, in the "Medical Group of Bossey" of which she called herself the concerned mother, then grandmother, and finally in the conference and apostolate journeys. Our greatest privilege was in having all these experiences, in living this great venture in the faith together, profoundly united, searching together, step by step, in the realization that God abided in us. So today, if my sorrow is great, my gratitude is even greater still. She would also express sincere thanks to all who surrounded me with their kindness.

—PAUL TOURNIER

DOROTHY: THE PRODIGAL DAUGHTER

I was absolutely enthralled the other day as I read an article by my friend Jack Exum entitled "The Story of the Loving Brother." In it, Jack tells the familiar story of the Prodigal Son found in Luke 15:11-32 with a unique twist.

Instead of the elder brother becoming angry at his younger brother for squandering their father's wealth in wild living, he leaves the safety of hearth and home to go look for him. The focus of the story, as told by Jack, is not on the Prodigal Son but on the Loving Brother who does whatever it takes to bring the prodigal home.

The elder brother decided to do something before it was too late. Going to his father he said, "Father, I can no longer stand by and watch death overtake you. We have heard of the famine that has struck the country where my brother went. I have packed my things, and with your blessings and prayers, I must go and find my brother. He is there, I know he is. I must go and bring him back home."

So he did. He left his father standing in that familiar spot, where each evening he would stand and watch and wait for his youngest son to return. But this time he watched as his oldest son slowly disappeared over the horizon. The journey was long and hard, but eventually he reached the land he sought. Then the search began in earnest "Have you seen my brother?" he would ask, again and again. He went door to door, house to house, and even throughout all of the "red-light" district. He loudly called him by name as he passed down each street. Finally he came to the house of his brother's master.

"Yes, I know him. I hired him about three months ago to feed my herd of swine. He is out in the field. Go, you'll find him there."

As the older brother climbed one of the rocky hills, his eyes beheld a scene worse than he could have imagined. There sat a man, much older than his years, in tattered rags, no shoes or sandals, covered with filth, his hair matted. Gaunt and broken, he sat gnawing one of the husks upon which the swine fed.

"Brother!" he cried, "I'm here, and I've come to take you home!"

They ran to meet each other, embraced and wept. "I knew you would come," the prodigal said, "I just knew you would come!"

The journey back seemed a much shorter path, filled with talk of home. They arrived about sunset. As they came over the last hill they could see standing, but somewhat stooped, the figure of a man. When they were clearly in sight, both brothers were amazed at what they witnessed. It was an absolute tradition that an old man would never run to greet a guest. But these were no guests, these were his sons. Only one issue was important: "Both my sons are home!" And he ran and gathered them both to his heart and wept.

Then a party began that surpassed all parties of all time. The fatted calf was killed. Neighbors came from far and near. Dancing and rejoicing filled the house, for one son was lost and was found by his brother. One son was dying and was rescued by a family's love.[4]

Many of you may have a lost sister or brother, father or mother, daughter or son. Like Auntie Em in *The Wizard of Oz*, maybe you've even called aloud for them to come back home. Unfortunately, Dorothy couldn't hear Auntie Em's cries. She was simply too far away. Sometimes—more often than not—*you just have to go get them*, don't you? You have to "quit praying long enough," concludes Exum, "to go find them." Before it's too late!

RESCUED BY A FAMILY'S LOVE AND PRAYERS

Let's examine another prodigal situation which brings up the question of how far the values of family extend. It brings up the need for faith and trust.

I sat in a cafe in north Atlanta with a friend who told me about his drug-addicted son.

"He called the other night," my friend began.

"Tell me about it."

"Well, he said he didn't have any money.... He was hungry.... He just wanted some money so he could eat a decent meal."

"What did you say?"

"I told him that we didn't do that anymore—send him money, that is. You know, the co-dependency thing? We didn't

---

[4] Jack Exum, "The Story of the Loving Brother," *Image* (July/August 1993), 22.

want to enable him to continue making the wrong choices. He's got to be responsible"

"I understand."

"But I..." My friend paused, choosing his words carefully as he choked back the tears. "I just want to get in my car—you know?—and go get him. Bring him back home where he belongs."

I'm sure some of you have struggled in the same way. To "rescue" someone these days is such risky business. There's got to be a limit, we reason. Why, we have to draw the line somewhere, right? Organizations like "Tough Love" recognize this dilemma and the immense pain it causes parents to have to decide whether or not to bail a son or daughter out for the hundredth time. Sometimes prodigals just have to learn it for themselves.

SHE WOULDN'T HAVE BELIEVED ME

It's kind of like when Dorothy is unintentionally left behind by the Wizard of Oz when the balloon takes off without her. Glenda comes and tells her that she always had the power to go home.

"Then why didn't you tell her?" asks the Tin Man.

"Because she wouldn't have believed me. She had to learn it for herself."

So it goes with life in the real world. Some people never learn, do they? They go right on doing the same destructive things—again and again, until some flash of insight comes and brings them back to their senses. It's that "ah-ha" experience—when the light goes on and you finally realize the folly of your ways.

I guess that's what happened to Dorothy. It wasn't enough for her to want to see her Uncle Henry or Auntie Em. She had to endure that whole process of finding a way to get back home. She had to struggle. She had to learn something.

Perhaps there's something to be learned in the struggle. We wrestle with ourselves. We rationalize.

We make excuses... until we finally run out of them and face the true reasons for the choices we've made.

But I think there are some prodigals who are legitimately stuck over the rainbow and just can't find their way home. *For them, a family's love may be their only hope.* Perhaps it is their only means of escape.

WE'VE GOT TO GET HER OUT!

Remember when Dorothy was trapped in the castle of the Wicked Witch? The Tin Man, assisted by the Lion and the Scarecrow, used his ax to break through the chamber door—something Dorothy could not have done by herself. She needed something more powerful. Sometimes our loved ones are held equally captive and need something more powerful—a *family's love and prayers.*

The things I'm going to share next may be a bit new for

some and old hat for others. Regardless, I share them because I believe them to be biblical.

In the Bible we are told that our "struggle is not against flesh and blood" (Eph. 6:12). "But against... the spiritual forces of evil." Where? The Bible states: "... in the heavenly realms."

It is my belief that some of our kin are actually trapped by these "spiritual forces of evil." These forces by nature are spiritual instead of physical and therefore invisible to the naked eye—but fortunately, not invisible to God. God sees them and is ready to pounce on them with our prayers!

Elsewhere in the Bible, we are told that prayer is a powerful weapon against these unseen forces of wickedness. "Pray in the Spirit on all occasions," reminds Paul, "with all kinds of prayers and requests" (Eph. 6:18). It is this "praying in the Spirit" that, according to prominent theologian J. Oswald Sanders, transacts its business in the sphere of the supernatural. Removed from the realm of the unassisted human mind, our prayers—assisted by the Holy Spirit—occupy a strategic role "through which the victory gained on Calvary over Satan and his hosts reaches the captives and delivers them."[5]

Now, I know some of us are uncomfortable with the term "deliverance." But, believe me, when you've tried every other method known to humankind, God's way is the best way; and for some, it is perhaps the only way to get back home again.

As for my friend in Atlanta, that's exactly what he did.

[5] J. Oswald Sanders, *Spiritual Leadership* (Chicago: Moody Press, 1980), 129.

Running out of options, he and his wife and one of their ministers got together for prayer to allow God's spirit to intercede for them. Armed with prayer and the Word of God, the minister met alone with the young prodigal and delivered him—that's right!—delivered him from the bondage of an "evil force." Their son was immediately restored to his "right mind." He could see clearly now—more clearly than ever before—the way back home, thanks to an unbeatable combination of *a family's love and prayers.*

HE'LL SEE THEM HOME

Don't despair so of your children,
God will bring them to the fold—
Because He died to save them,
They're special to the Lord.
He knows how much you love them,
He loves them even more.
As long as you hold on in prayer,
He'll not close the door.
Even now He sees your tears,
And He whispers tenderly,
Of love that conquered all—
That all men might be free.
So lay them at His altar,
Let go and leave them there—
God will be faithful to your trust,

He won't withhold His care.
His hand will ever nurture,
No matter where they roam—
And He won't be satisfied
'Til He sees them safely home!

—JOYCE HENNING

ALL THINGS LOST: SHEEP, COINS, AND KIN

God knows the pain of things lost. His joy is greater still when He finds them. It's hard for us to imagine God, like desperate parents, searching every nook and cranny for those who have gone astray. Yet He does! Ours is a God whose emotions run deep. Greater love has no one—remember? And this love is seen not only in his death on the cross, but in his life's search for the prodigals who have wandered away from home.

To drive home this point, I suggest that Luke's Gospel provides three parables of Jesus that, according to Scottish New Testament interpreter, William Barclay, contain "the very distilled essence of the good news which Jesus came to tell."[6] Barclay continues:

These parables arose out of definite situations. It was an offense to the scribes and Pharisees that Jesus associated with

[6] William Barclay, *The Gospel According to Luke: The Daily Bible Study Series* (Philadelphia: Westminister Press, 1975), 199.

men and women who, by the orthodox, were labeled as sinners. The Pharisees gave to people who did not keep the law a general classification. They called them the People of the Land; and there was a complete barrier between the Pharisees and the People of the Land. To marry a daughter to one of them was the exposing her bound and helpless to a lion. The Pharisaic regulations laid it down, "When a man is one of the People of the Land, entrust no money to him, take no testimony from his, trust him with no secret, do not appoint him guardian of an orphan, do not make him the custodian of charitable funds, do not accompany him on a journey." A Pharisee was forbidden to be the guest of any such man or to have him as his guest. He was even forbidden, so far as it was possible, to have any business dealings with him. It was deliberate Pharisaic aim to avoid every contact with the people who did not observe the petty details of the law. Obviously, they would be shocked to the core at the way in which Jesus companied with people who were not only rank outsiders, but sinners, contact with those who would necessarily defile. We will understand these parables more fully if we remember that the strict Jews said, not "There will be joy in heaven over one sinner who repents," but, "There will be joy in heaven over one sinner who is obliterated before God." They looked sadistically forward not to the saving but to the destruction of the sinner.[7]

Jesus told them the parables of the lost sheep, coin, and

[7] Ibid., 199-200.

151

kin to help us all understand the "tremendous truth that God is kinder than men."[8] Men may give up on the prodigals of this world; not so God, concludes Barclay. "It is a thousand times easier to come back to God than to come home to the bleak criticism of men."[9]

There is also the realization that at some point, we have to hand over our lost loved ones to God.

Ruth Bell Graham wrote a poem that expresses well our need to trust God's sovereignty. "Our ways are not His ways," we must admit, and ultimately surrender in prayer to the truth that lies deep within our souls—God is God and we are not.

She waited for the call
that never came;
searched every mail
for a letter,
or a note,
or card,
that bore his name;
and on her knees
at night,
and on her feet
all day,
she stormed Heaven's Gate
in his behalf,'

[8] Ibid., 201.
[9] Ibid.

she pleaded for him
in Heaven's high court.
"Be still and wait; and see" —
the word God gave; then she
knew that He would
do in and for and with him,
that which she could never do.
So Doubts ignored
she went about her chores
with you—
knowing though spurned,
His word was true.
The prodigal had not returned,
but God was God,
and there was work to do.[10]

This is the conclusion of the matter, writes Ruth Bell Graham: "As a mother, I must faithfully, patiently, lovingly and happily do my part—then quietly wait for God to do His."[11] Quoting Psalm 27:18 from the Anglican Prayer Book—"O, tarry thou the Lord's leisure..."—she says in parting, "And He is so leisurely at times!"

When reflecting on "The Prodigal Son," William Barclay tells the story of President Abraham Lincoln, who one day "was asked how he was going to treat the rebellious south-

[10] Ruth Bell Graham, *Prodigals and Those Who Love Them* (Colorado Springs: Focus on the Family, 1991), 132.
[11] Ibid., 24.

erners when they had finally been defeated and had returned to the Union of the United States."

"I will treat them," said Lincoln, "like they had never been away."[12]

Upon our return, God treats us like we had never gone astray!

This is the wonder of Him. You see, God's love always precedes forgiveness. It is because He loves us that we are forgiven. Barclay is right: God's love defeats our foolishness, the seduction of the tempting voices, and even the deliberate rebellion of the human heart.[13] This is the message of the three parables of Christ. And this is the hope for our future: Our "children shall come again to their own border" (Jer. 31:17).

Eventually we all must go home, as the following poem eloquently expresses.

FOOLISH CHILDREN

Waking in the night to pray,
Sleeping when the answer comes,
Foolish are we even at play—
Tearfully we beat our drums!
Cast the good dry bread away,
Weep, and gather up the crumbs!

[12] William Barclay, *The Gospel According to Luke: The Daily Bible Study Series* (Philadelphia: Westminister Press, 1975), 205.

[13] Ibid., 206.

"Evermore," while shines the day,
"Lord," we cry, "thy will be done!"
Soon as evening groweth gray,
Thy fair will we fain would shun!
"Take, oh, take thy hand away!
See the horrid dark begun!"
"Thou hast conquered death," we say,
"Christ, whom Hades could not keep!"
Then, "Ah, see the pallid clay!
Death it is," we cry, "Not sleep!
Grave, take all. Shut out the day.
Sit we on the ground and weep!"

Gathering potsherds all the day,
Truant children, Lord, we roam;
Fret, and longer wait to play,
When at cool thy voice doth come!—
Elder Brother, lead the way,'
Make us good as we go home.

—GEORGE MACDONALD[14]

[14] George MacDonald, *Discovering the Character of God*, ed. Michael R. Phillips (Minneapolis: Bethany House Publishers, 1989), 182.

PART FOUR

Working through the Trials of Oz: How We Get Contentment

Sometimes values are not acted out in life without our first having to go through trials, without enduring some tests. Contentment doesn't necessarily come to us because we are good and have a solid set of values. We usually learn the importance of acting out those values by seeing what life is like without them, and by seeing and being tempted by opposing values.

Part Four deals with how to work through those trials and tests, and how to find the contentment we all seek. True contentment comes from home and family—at the beginning of the rainbow. But we must usually go somewhere over the rainbow—through Oz—in order to come home again. Chapter 10 treats the process of God's ways occurring in twisters, in the necessity of trials; it also presents helpful prescriptions for our restless hearts that keep us moving toward God. Chapter 11 discusses coming home and three necessary movements we must take to get there. Chapter 12 concludes by presenting concepts of community and accountability as essential to completing the process of coming home from Oz.

TEN

God's Way is in Twisters:
Prescriptions for
the Restless Heart

The first step toward home is to put God in the center of the process. He keeps our hearts in a state of restlessness for just that purpose. This chapter first looks at the essence of this process—restlessness—and then gives four useful prescriptions for the restless heart.

In the Old Testament there is a saying: God's "way is in

the whirlwind and the storm" (Neh. 1:3). Yet it's difficult to comprehend why God's voice is more easily heard during times of great pain and suffering. It is often said that God's best work is accomplished in the "refining fires" that come our way—those unexpected disasters that force us to stop, listen, and learn.

We see this in *The Wizard of* Oz, don't we? It took a whirlwind and a storm to teach Dorothy and her family that to lose those whom we love is to be thrown into a discontentment of tornado-like proportions. How miserable we are until we finally yield to the lesson: God's "will be done in earth as it is in heaven" (Matt. 6:10).

As in the case of Dorothy and her family, God's will has to do with human relationships. This is the source of our greatest discontent—to be unreconciled to God and each other! Subsequently, this is the prayer of the Divine: that we would all be one, as the Father and the Son are one (see John 17:20-21). Robert Schuller discusses this special prayer in the following way:

A simple and very wise man once said: "If you really want to know a person's deepest desire and most conscientious concern, study, if you can, his unvarnished prayers. Stealthily approach him in his intimate closet and try to overhear what he is really praying about passionately."

If we are then courageous, humble, and sincere enough to

discover our Lord's imperative for his followers today, we can hardly go wrong by studying the prayer that Christ gave to his disciples and to us with the suggestion that we pray daily. Surely, we can expect Christ's divine directive to be contained within the substance of the prayer that he gave us. I suggest then that we can discover that Christ will reveal his deepest concern for you, for me, and for all believers today if we will study the prayer that down through the centuries has been called "The Lord's Prayer."

What is our Lord's greatest passion for his church today? I believe that he wants his followers to respect themselves as equal children of God and to treat all other human beings with that same respect.

"Our Father" is a call to be a family, and it is an invitation to find our pride in belonging to God's family. So, what would Jesus say if he could speak to us today? Would he tell us what miserable sinners we are? I think not.

Deep down in our hearts I believe we know that Jesus would say something like this to us: "You are the salt of the earth. You are the light of the world. You are a child of the Eternal. Follow Me and I will make you fishers of men."

Receive and enjoy the fruit of salvation: self-esteem, self-worth. Hear God's call to you. He would save you for high and holy service—to be proud of who you are. Then, stop putting yourself down. Start enjoying the dignity that is your God-intended destiny.[1]

As I've stated before, I believe Dr. Schuller is right on target when he suggests that God's ultimate will for us is to have the right kind of relationships as his family, and that from this family ought to come a dignity that is our God-intended destiny. Imagine, concludes Schuller, how society can be prevented from "a myriad mixture of human tragedies resulting from persons consumed by their 'ego' problems" if we found our fulfillment and our heart's contentment "satisfied in a beautiful relationship with Christ and his family."[2] I couldn't agree more! But often finding that relationship with God involves twisters... discontentment.

A young man who attends the church where I minister shared a good example of a "twister" with me over lunch one day. It is one of the most remarkable true stories I have ever heard. He told me that when he was only eleven years old he climbed an eighty-foot water tower with a friend. Due to the ice and snow the climb was particularly treacherous, and getting off the tower ladder to slide down some support bars made things even worse. Needless to say, he fell.

I couldn't believe my ears as he recounted all of the horrible details. Especially unbelievable was the fact that he

[1] Robert H. Schuller, *Self-Esteem: The New Reformation* (Waco, TX: Word Incorporated, 1982), 46-47.

[2] Ibid., 47.

survived. How does one fall from a incredibly high tower to the hard, icy ground below and live to tell the tale? It was clear that God had a purpose in sparing his life that cold winter day.

My friend explained that he came from a fairly unloving home. When he was a little boy his mother committed suicide. A cold and indifferent stepmother proved a poor substitute for a child who needed the love of a mother, now more than ever. Climbing the tower became his only means of escape. Up there, seemingly above the clouds, he felt free.

All that changed, of course, and the very place that had once provided him refuge from a tortured childhood sent him crashing to the earth below. "I didn't care if I died," he confessed. Living recklessly was his way of coping with a lack of love.

He told me he hit the ground so hard that he literally bounced five feet in the air. "I crushed both ankles and broke some ribs." But that wasn't the worst of it: "I also had internal bleeding and complications due to pneumonia." The doctors said he probably wouldn't live and in the unlikely event he did survive, would never walk again!

He would prove them wrong on both counts.

"As I lay there in a hospital bed for three months, I began to think about all the things I was doing to hurt God and my family. By saving my life, God showed me that I was worth something; and oddly enough, he showed my parents—my step-mom and dad—that I was worth something to them too.

Why, it took an eighty-foot, near-fatal fall to unite me to God; and eventually, unite me to my family. I have never been the same since."

Ruth Bell Graham addresses such a process in the following poem:

> It is a fearful thing to fall into Your hands, O living God!
> Yet I must trust to You my all, praying your staff and
> rod will comfort each in need as well as break the
> wayward leg. And yet I plead
> "Deal gently with the young man
> for my sake."[3]

PRESCRIPTIONS FOR THE RESTLESS HEART

Fulfillment for the restless heart comes from knowing God.

In his best-selling book, A *Second Touch*, Keith Miller identifies this same restlessness and suggests that a relationship with God is the answer. A former businessman himself, Miller examines his own frantic search for something or someone to quiet his restlessness. Although he concludes that God is the fulfillment for his restless heart, he challenges us to consider the probability that this anxiousness will never leave us and quite possibly it is God's design to "force us to grow as Christians." He writes:

[3] Ruth Bell Graham, *Prodigals and Those Who Love Them* (Colorado Springs: Focus on the Family, 1991), 107.

As Christians, we have realized that this universal existential need is a built-in or instinctive need for God and other people, which will not let man rest short of the deep completion and relatedness for which he was made. It was this sense of relatedness which I was realizing in my new relationship with Christ and with people around me. At a profound level I knew the big search for meaning and security was over, even though I still had uncertain and unsettled times. As Augustine described this universal dependency need in Christian terms: "Thou madest us for thyself, and our heart is restless, until it repose in thee."

In wrestling with my anxiousness as a Christian, I saw that this restless desire which drives us to God causes a great deal of our anxiety as human beings. There is a fear that our deepest need will not be met. In fact some people have told me in anguish that they were afraid to really commit their lives to God for fear that he would not be real, and then what would they do. So they "keep him alive" by keeping their distance, since they could not endure a world without the hope, however remote, that their deepest and most haunting needs would be met. Since the relationship with God and his people has begun to fill this deepest existential vacuum for millions of men and women, many people in the church have unconsciously assumed that when one truly begins the Christian life, the anxiety should disappear forever. And its presence after conversion is a sign of a relative falling back into an uncommitted state.

But now I was finding that we do not shuck off this deep need just because we become Christians. In fact, this drive is the recurring hunger that now forces us to grow as Christians. When I accepted Christ as Lord and Savior (from the hopeless quest of living without God), this deepest need in my life was arrested. I felt free from the frantic nature of the basic "driveness" of life. Having a great purpose now, I set out to live this life through the disciplines, etc., which seemed to go along with it. But then, when I began to "conquer the disciplines," I started unconsciously not to depend on God and his people but on my acquired knowledge about these things. My dependence was once again in my ability; only this time my religious ability, and not in the strengthening love and power of God. Getting to be known by a few Christians, I was being depended on and felt that I must be religious and strong, not anxious and weak—when truth is that I often am anxious and weak. But I had subtly put myself in God's place again, to be for other people that which they needed—God. But he is the only One who can meet our basic dependency needs. He designed them. And I had become anxious and incomplete again because I had conquered the techniques and was unconsciously on the hunt once more for a deeper security than they provided. At last this search sent me to my knees as a child, where I would again put my life in his hands. For me then, Christian restlessness was not necessarily bad, but, like physical pain, it could be a warning signal—warning me that something was overloaded in my life, that something was out of balance. And because of the signal which anxiety provided, I could stop and do something before I destroyed myself.

When I realized that man's existential sense of dependency and periodic anxious restlessness are a part of the fabric of Christian living, I was quietly awed. Instead of driving me away from Christianity, as this discovery has some of my "God is dead" (or seriously wounded) friends, I was thrilled. Because this discovery—that my restlessness is there to get my attention and point me back toward Christ—freed me as I have never been freed to be human as a Christian. If my faith is in God, then my job is not to build a successful, untainted religious life; it is to live a joyous and creative human life. I am to love him, love his people and love living, as poor and incomplete as I am or ever will be—yet free not to have to be a God-shaped wooden saint. My recurring restlessness is a natural part of life, driving me ever deeper in my relationship with him. I found that the more my ultimate trust was in God, the less I tended to be involved in neurotic dependency relationships with people. And I saw how Jesus could live trustingly among men but not lay the burden of his primary trust on them, knowing they could not fulfill it (John 2:24). And in some way which I could not understand, the more ultimately I was dependent on God and not ashamed to be weak, the more power I seemed to have to help people.[4]

This "recurring restlessness" of which Miller speaks is no doubt the same dynamic that causes men and women to leave their homes—even their marriages—in search for something more. The "drivenness" that he describes destroys many families. Thus, returning to one's family without dealing with the root cause of such drivenness is likely to produce the same result of indifference or abandonment as before.

Only God can be the answer, with our families being an environment where God is continually experienced, where everyday God is discovered anew: where the search for something more is satisfied every time the family prays together, experiences God's grace together, sees God's miracles together, and participates in his divine character by forgiving each other as they have been forgiven. His presence will be there—to be experienced and discovered and embraced every day—in the holiest of institutions if all family members are taught to view the home as *sacred* in the eyes of God.

The sacredness of the home, however, does not exist apart from the presence of God; but that sacredness is present in family relationships when two or three are gathered in Christ's name and God is in the midst of them (see Matt. 18:20). Thus, self-interest must be replaced by a spiritual interest in the family that includes making God real by a mutual submission out of reverence for Christ (see Eph.5:21)

[4] Keith Miller, A *Second Touch* (Waco, TX: Word Publishing, 1967), 64-66.

My restless heart is fulfilled when, as a husband, I experience God every day in the act of loving my wife "just as Christ loved the church and gave himself up for her" (Eph. 5:25). It is fulfilled when a wife submits to her husband, as to the Lord (see Eph. 5:22). It is fulfilled when a child obeys his parents and honors his father and mother (see Eph.6: 1-2). It is fulfilled, when as a father, I don't exasperate my children; "instead, bring them up in the training and instruction of the Lord" (Eph. 6:4). Four prescriptions for restless hearts help us along the path. They involve being filled with the Spirit, rejoicing in the Lord always, bringing our prayers and petitions to God, and thinking about what is Godlike and putting it into practice.

BE FILLED WITH THE SPIRIT

To be in submission—or "subject to one another" (RSV)—depends on the Bible's earlier command, "be filled with the Spirit" (Eph. 5:18). Submission, then, is a natural and inevitable by-product of the Holy Spirit's fullness in our lives. It is important to understand that if God is to be made manifest or real among us, his character must fill up our lives. The fruit of the Spirit, as recorded in Galatians, chapter 5,. promotes a right—or righteous—relationship with God and others. In order for this fruit to be exhibited in our lives we must first submit to God. God's fruit, then, comes out of our submission to him. in turn, his fruit or character fills us up and enables us to submit to one another—empowering us to "speak to one another with psalms, hymns and spiritual songs" (Eph. 5:19).

There can be nothing more fulfilling in our lives than to experience the personal work of the Holy Spirit in each other. Since it is the intention of the Holy Spirit to promote fellowship, ministry to one another, and a building up of the body of Christ, there can be no doubt that to "be filled with the Holy Spirit" is to be others-centered versus self-centered. By bringing the Holy Spirit into our lives we are at once availing ourselves of a relationship-building dynamic that may have previously eluded us.

We often ignore the work of the Holy Spirit to our peril and believe that merely psychology or some other philosophical approach to life will change us and those whom we love. But true and lasting change is always found in the realm of the miraculous—where the "crucified Servant-Messiah" exists, says theologian Markus Barth.

> When a person is voluntarily amenable to another, gives way to him, and places himself at his service, he shows greater dignity and freedom than an individual who cannot bear to be a helper and partner to anyone but himself. Ephesians 5 shows that in [this] realm, the subjects respect an order of freedom and equality in which one person assists another—seemingly by renouncing rights possessed, actually in exercising the right to imitate the Messiah himself.... A greater, wiser, and more

positive description of marriage has not yet been found in Christian literature.[5]

REJOICE IN THE LORD ALWAYS

The exhortation of the Bible is to be cheerful (see Phil. 4:4). Cheerfulness acknowledges the work of grace in the life of the believer. It is because Christ has saved us that we ought to be glad and bring such gladness into our homes for all the world to see (see Acts 2:46b). Those who are cheerful have a predisposition to unity and cohesion with other family members. Why, they're just plain easier to be around!

Those who are constantly critical often are the least cheerful and, by contrast, are the most difficult to be around. Dale Carnegie, author of the best-selling book, *How to Win Friends and Influence People*, taught that if you wanted a happier home then you should curb your tongue and give-up "futile, heartbreaking criticism." To drive home his point, Carnegie writes about William and Katherine Gladstone and "the supreme happiness of their private lives."

[They] lived together for forty-nine years, almost three score years glorified with an abiding devotion. I like to think of Gladstone, the most dignified of England's prime ministers, clasping his wife's hand and dancing around the hearthrug with her, singing this song:

"A ragamuffin husband and a rantipoling wife, We'll fiddle it

[5] Markus Barth, *The Broken Wall* (Collins, 1960), 714-715.

and scrape it through the ups and downs of life."

Gladstone, a formidable enemy in public, never criticized at home. When he came down to breakfast in the morning, only to discover the rest of his family was still sleeping, he had a gentle way of registering his reproach. He raised his voice and filled the house with a mysterious chant that reminded the other members that England's busiest man was waiting downstairs for his breakfast, all alone. Diplomatic, considerate, he rigorously refrained from domestic criticism.[6]

In contrast to harsh criticism, the Bible simply concludes, "Let your gentleness be evident to all" (Phil. 4:5). Such forbearance or reasonableness, expressed in rejoicing and in our gentleness with family members, is another by-product of God's Spirit filling us up. It will be such filling up that will surely empower us to win friends and influence family.

BRING YOUR PRAYERS AND PETITIONS TO GOD

After one of my seminars an anxious parent came up to me and asked, "What are the three most important things I should do on a daily basis to be an effective parent?" I quickly responded: "Pray. Pray. And, then, pray some more." We both smiled.

Charles Stanley has written a book, Handle With Prayer, in

---

[6] Dale Carnegie, How to Win Friends and Influence People (New York: Pocket Books, 1964), 222.

which he says that many Christians are top-notch worriers and mediocre prayers. He suggests that we tune our spiritual ears to God's leading with the absolute assurance he will answer us. "... Some answers will only be found in prayer," he writes, "not from other sources—not from books, not from friends, and not from counselors."[7] He continues:

Some things must come straight from God, the Source of all wisdom. How many families would still be together today if they had sought God's answers to their problems at home? How many sons and daughters would still be home if their parents had taken their situation to the Lord? But often we refuse to wait on God's answers. We want quick solutions to our problems.

But God wants to do much more than just meet our needs and answer our questions. He wants our love. He wants our spirits. He wants our lives. Yes, He encourages us to bring our trials and our heartaches to Him in prayer, but only after we recognize who He is and what He can do. Only then do we believe He will answer our prayers. Only then are we seeking His face, and not merely His hands.[8]

I can attest to the power of prayer in the life of a family. After our daughter Cara died, the hospital expenses were set up in a payment plan so we could financially handle the

[7] Charles Stanley, *Handle With Prayer* (Wheaton, IL: Victor Books, 1984), 14.
[8] Ibid., 14-15.

burden. Unfortunately, the billing system at the hospital went haywire and began listing us as delinquent even though we had paid our bills on time. Needless to say, it was painful to come home from work only to find another threatening notice from another bill collector for the hospital. After several phone calls to the hospital, the delinquency notices stopped.

Then one day I came home for lunch to find my wife in tears. It seems that this time our name was sent to a lawyer for collections. Obviously, the lawyer—representing his client, the hospital—was even less kind. He threatened to sue us if we didn't pay the remainder of our bill immediately. This threw my wife into absolute despair. Not only had we just buried our daughter, but now we were being harassed. It was more than I could bear.

So I decided to call the hospital one last time, and when that didn't work—I hit the ceiling!

By now furious, I decided to go down to the hospital and "bang some heads." My wife and young son looked on with horror as I stomped angrily out of the house. But God stopped me. As I noticed the expressions on my son's and wife's faces, I began to see what a fool I had been. Taking them into my arms, I knelt down and began to pray for God to intercede. I acknowledged that his way was the best way and handed my request over to him with thanksgiving.

Within minutes, the phone rang.

Rachel answered it. It was the hospital calling back.

"Don't send another dime, Mrs. O'Donnell. Your bill has been paid in full." We couldn't believe our ears. The hospital had canceled our bill. Over a thousand dollars. We ran to each other in tears, praising God—never to doubt that God hears and answers our prayers!

> Do not be anxious about anything, but in everything, by prayer and petition, with thanksgiving, present your request to God. And the peace of God, which transcends all understanding, will guard your hearts and minds in Christ Jesus (Phil. 4:6-7).

THINK ABOUT WHAT IS NOBLE, RIGHT, PURE, LOVELY, ADMIRABLE, OR EXCELLENT AND PUT IT INTO PRACTICE.

> Finally, brothers, whatever is true, whatever is noble, whatever is right, whatever is pure, whatever is lovely, whatever is admirable—if anything is excellent or praiseworthy—think about such things. Whatever you have learned from me [Paul], or seen in me—put into practice. And the God of peace will be with you (Phil. 4:8-9).

The Bible is saying we should let our minds dwell on good things and not the bad things of this world. This reminds me of the hand-sewn plaque my wife, Rachel, put on top of the television set one day. It simply read: "I will set before my eyes no vile thing" (Ps. 10:3). And that's not all she did.

Having gotten home from a Focus on the Family seminar on the negative effects of television, she came in on the most sacred of all evenings: Monday Night Football. She unplugged the TV and turned it around to face the corner. My dad, who had been watching the game with me, turned and said, "Uhm, Michael, she's your wife." I asked, "What are you doing, Rachel?"

Quick came the reply: "Well, it's like this—when Patrick is disobedient, I put him in the corner. So, until the TV says the things I want to hear and does the things I want it to do, then, just like with Patrick, *it's staying in the corner!*" She had a point.

The Bible is telling us that if we don't want our inner contentment disturbed, then we should keep our minds on the things of God and not the things of earth (see Col. 3:2). We are also being asked to find out what is good, and with the help of the Holy Spirit, put it into practice in our homes.

I believe that if we take our daily dose of God's four prescriptions for the restless heart, then the drivenness of which Keith Miller writes will be harnessed and under God's control. We will be driven to please God and each other. We will strive to outdo one another in love and by this the world will know we are Christians.

As we make our final journey home from over the rainbow, those who would find contentment might once again hear what Keith Miller has to say:

My own experience and investigation has led me to believe that committing my life as wholly as I can to God and receiving the reassuring sense of His Holy Spirit does give me a deep and ultimate security my humanity has longed for. But, when one discovers that he is again anxious as a Christian, he can know that Christ counted on His disciples having troubled hearts and told them He was sending the Holy Spirit to comfort or "strengthen" them when they did (see John 14). So I have come to see that restlessness and ultimate dependency, like pain and evil, are woven into the fabric of life and that Christ does not abolish these for the Christian, but periodically they may become the motive power to drive us toward fulfillment in Him.[9]

[9] Miller, 69-70.

Eleven

Coming Home

In coming home we will find that the movement of our restless hearts upward toward God initiates two other movements: a movement inward toward self and a movement outward toward others. This chapter examines these three steps toward home.

SOFTLY AND TENDERLY HE CALLS

Dr. Ken Kennedy, professor emeritus at Kansas State

University, tells an interesting story of one husband's journey home. Here is the story of Kevin:

At age thirty Kevin was a broken man.

Success had come early to him. He had been a leader on campus and in a nationally touring singing group while in college. Academic success, with several graduate degrees and published papers, followed quickly. When he took his first full-time job, the company that hired him sprang forth with new life and enthusiasm, along with rapid growth in sales. But at the same time his marriage was falling apart.

He could scarcely believe that it was really him when he found himself in an adulterous relationship. Kevin thought he was too smart, too in control, and too above reproach to let that happen. But it happened. His wife divorced him. Now the tightly held cord of pride and self confidence that made him a cocky, aggressive, "I'll-do-it-my-way" kind of guy began to unravel.

Devastated beyond words and at complete rock bottom, Kevin contemplated suicide. It was then that he encountered the invitation, "Come to me, you who are weary and burdened, and I will give you rest" (Matt. 11:28).

Overwhelmed, vulnerable, and now open, he accepted the

total, unconditional forgiveness of God. Kevin experienced an unexplainable joy and contentment he had never known before.

Now remarried and with several children to love, Kevin relies on God, not the world, for answers. He also meets once a week with a men's prayer group that has breathed new life into his once broken heart. "This small group of men," concludes Kevin, "showed me the way home!"

THREE STEPS TOWARD HOME

Just like Dorothy had to click her heels three times to find herself back home, so we need to consider three things that when focused upon will achieve the same effect. Although the above illustration is gender specific, the concept of embracing God's call to return home and enter into a covenant with persons who care is not. Both men and women need Jesus in their lives and same-sex friendships that will enable them to move upward toward God, inward toward self, and outward toward others.

UPWARD TOWARD GOD

The first step in returning home is establishing a relationship with God. This relationship begins with one clear, concise condition: "love the Lord your God with all your heart and with all your soul and with all your mind and with all your might" (Deut. 6:5). Such a condition assumes that our loving God will change your life. Because we are being asked to love Him with our *all*—that is, everything we are physically, spiritually, emotionally, and mentally—little room is left over for anything else. God, then, and not money, status, or success becomes the object of our life's affections. We no longer define who we are in terms of what we own, or know, or even what we can do, but solely in terms of to whom we belong! We begin by loving the One in whose image we have been created (see Gen. 1:27).

Just think about it. Each of us resembles God in the ability to have the same kind of love he has for his creation and to form familial relationships that will literally last forever. If your heart has been far from God or caught up in the things of this world, then such eternal relationships with self and others become impossible. We cannot move inward toward self or outward toward others until we have moved upward toward "him who is able to do immeasurably more than all we ask or imagine" (Eph. 3:20).

Now if you're like me, you're probably thinking that you can ask for and imagine quite a lot. But God who created you can surpass human desires and imagination.

Sometimes we imagine that being in a new marriage or family will bring us the joy we lack, or having more money, more fame, more this or that. We imagine more is better, right? But people who have achieved their goals tell us they still lack something to make them whole and happy beings.

What is it that they still lack to have the contentment they seek? A *relationship with God*!

Many who desire better looks, less weight, more smarts discover that when they finally get that long awaited nose job, body beautiful, or Ph.D. they still want more. When is enough... *enough*? You know the answer: enough is never enough. What is it that we really desire, then? A *relationship with God*! Until we have a relationship with God, all the black bags of the many millions of wizards the world over will never contain what we truly hunger for. Jesus knew this. Remember when Satan, the definitive Wicked Witch, tempted Jesus with food to fill his hungry belly? Jesus proclaimed that it was a relationship with God and not the temporary things of this world that fills one up (see Matt. 4:4).

This is ultimately the lesson that the rich young ruler learned in Matthew 19:16-24. He had great wealth, great status, and great power; yet he asked Jesus: "What do I still lack?" In essence, Jesus said, "You lack me! I am your only way to having the contentment you seek! It is me and not the things of this world you must possess!" It is this sole possession, not some magical, mythical Wizard of Oz, that will turn our hearts toward home and empower us to love and be loved.

Sally began to weep—silently at first, then aloud. "What is it?" asked her husband, now awake beside her. "I can't put my finger on it, Phil, it's just that I feel so empty inside. I have a great job, a beautiful house. I can't remember the last time I wanted something that I couldn't have or get. What's wrong with me? Why do I feel such discontent?"

Phil knew the answer but was afraid his response would seem trite. He longed to speak to her of his new found relationship with God, but feared appearing insensitive or overly religious. A question came to his mind. He began slowly: "Sally, where is your emptiness exactly?"

"My heart, Phil. It's my heart." She began to weep more heavily."

"I know that feeling, Sally. I had it, too. It's a longing for something or someone, right?"

"What are you getting at, Phil?"

Phil picked up a small book by Thomas a Kempis placed on their night stand for his evening devotional and began to read aloud:

Whatever I can desire or imagine for my comfort, I do not look for it here, but hereafter. For if I could have the comforts of this world, and enjoy all of its delights, it is certain that they could not last long. Wherefore you cannot, O my soul, be fully comforted, nor perfectly refreshed except in God, Who is the Comforter of the poor and the Defender of the humble. Wait a little, O my soul, wait for the Divine promise, and you shall have abundance of all good things in Heaven. If you unduly desire the things that are present, you will lose those 'which are eternal and heavenly. Use the temporal: desire the eternal. You cannot satisfy yourself with any temporal goods, because you were not created for the purpose of enjoying them.

Though you had all created goods, you could not be happy and blessed; but in God, Who made all things, your whole blessedness and felicity consist—not the kind of happiness which is approved and praised by the foolish lovers of this world, but such as the good and faithful of Christ look for, and of which the spiritual and pure in heart, whose conversation is in Heaven, sometimes enjoy a foretaste. Vain and brief is all human consolation. Blessed and true is that solace which is felt within from the Truth. A devout man carries with him every-where Jesus, his Comforter, and says to Him, "Be with me, O Lord Jesus, in every place and at all times. Let this be my consolation, to be quite willing to be without all human relief. And if Thy consolation be wanting, let Thy will and the trial I justly undergo, be for me my highest comfort."[1]

In the security of these words, Sally fell fast asleep.

INWARD TOWARD SELF

"There can be a state of the soul against which love itself is powerless," writes Gerald Vann, "because it has hardened itself against love." He expounds:

[1] Thomas A Kempis, *Of the Imitation of Christ* (Westwood, NJ: Fleming H. Revell Company, 1963) 35.

Hell is essentially a state of being which we fashion for ourselves: a state of final separateness from God which is the result not of God's repudiation of man, but of man's repudiation of God and a repudiation which is eternal precisely because it has become, in itself, immovable .... So with the soul and God; pride can become hardened into hell, hatred can become hardened into hell, any of the seven root forms of wrongdoing can harden into hell, and not least that sloth which is boredom with divine things, the inertia that cannot be troubled to repent, even though it sees the abyss into which the soul is falling, because for so long, in little ways perhaps, it has accustomed itself to refuse whatever might cost it an effort. May God in his mercy save us from that.[2]

Once we turn upward in our relationship to God we must let him move us and all that would be an invincible roadblock to a penetrating and convicting look into the human heart.

To be in the presence of God is to no longer stand immobile—paralyzed by suppressed or denied sin in our lives. It is to move toward dealing openly and honestly with those things that destroy family cohesion and unity and replace them with nothing less than the character of almighty God.

In this perpetual act of deep introspection and self-examination, we admit our powerlessness over stubborn, destructive habits of the heart and we acknowledge the only

[2] Gerald Vann, *The Pain of Christ and the Sorrow of God* (Springfield, IL: Temple Gate Publishing, 1982), 54-55.

One who can speak sufficiently to our human dilemma. "For all have sinned and fallen short of the glory of God," becomes a new spiritual reality that takes away our old, complacent, self directed idolatry and replaces it with a human dignity which flows from a right relationship with God.

For me, sin is nothing more than that which destroys human relationships and our relationship to God. God's righteousness or "right relationships," as I like to say, is the absence of sin in our lives. In God's Kingdom, sin is replaced with the fruit of his spirit or character.

Take the apostle Paul's letter to the church at Galatia, for example. In it he writes that "the acts of the sinful nature are obvious" and then he goes on to list them: "Sexual immorality, impurity and debauchery; idolatry and witch-craft; hatred, discord, jealousy, fits of rage, selfish ambition, dissensions, factions and envy; drunkenness, orgies, and the like" (Galatians 5:19-21). If you study the list carefully, I think you'll find a value system—with an attitude toward ambition, lifestyle, and family relationships that is at total odds with God's new society. This society, writes John R.W. Stott, "is characterized by life in place of death, by unity and reconcil-iation in place of division and alienation, by the wholesome standards of righteousness in place of hatred and strife, and by unremitting conflict with evil in place of a flabby compromise with it. "[3]

[3] John R.W. Stott, *God's New Society* (Downers Grove, IL: Inter-Varsity Press, 1979), author's preface.

This list found in Galatians, chapter 5, represents the kind of sins that we need to confess as damaging to the vitality and solidarity of the family group. Sexual immorality when expressed as adultery destroys trust. Fits of rage when taken to the extreme of spouse or child abuse destroy love. Drunkenness, hatred, and discord are all able to cause the breakdown of household relationships. But God knew this. He also knew we couldn't deal with these problems alone, that we needed help. Thus, God so loved the human "family"—remember, we're all blood relatives—"that he gave his one and only Son, that whoever believes in him shall not perish but have eternal life" (John 3:16).

But the life that is eternal is not only found after death! It begins today as the Holy Spirit brings us to a conviction of sin, to a vision of Christ's moral loveliness, and to a conversion and restoration of both heart and home.

Such a turning of our hearts toward home, by moving first upward toward God and secondly inward toward self, is no less than a conversion experience. No matter how reluctant you might be, you must allow God to move you to a point of repentance. It is the only hope to you and your family. By your turning away from sin you are returning from Oz and the yellow brick road down which you—like Dorothy—had gone astray. Consider the conversion experience of C. S. Lewis in his autobiographical narrative, *Surprised by Joy*. Although reluctant, he finally came home like a modern-day "Prodigal Son":

You must picture me alone in that room in Magdalen, night after night, feeling, whenever my mind lifted for a second from my work, the steady, unrelenting approach of Him whom I so earnestly desired not to meet. That which I greatly feared had at last come upon me. In the Trinity Term of 1929 I gave in, and admitted that God was God, and knelt and prayed: perhaps, that night, the most dejected and reluctant convert in all England. I did not then see what is now the most shining and obvious thing; the divine humility which will accept a convert even on such terms. The Prodigal Son at least walked home on his own feet. But who can duly adore that Love which will open the high gates to a prodigal who is brought in kicking, struggling, resentful, and darting his eyes in every direction for a chance to escape?... The hardness of God is kinder than the softness of men, and His compulsion is our liberation.[4]

Maybe your conversion experience will be or has been less sensational... but eventually all must "give in."

Conversion comes the moment when we realize that we've been following the wrong road—a yellow brick road. It doesn't take a wizard, ruby slippers, or three clicks of our heels to come home from Oz. All it takes is a simple faith in God and a willingness to move, with our "own two feet" or "kicking or struggling," toward a spiritual home of tender mercies. Yes, softly and tenderly we are being called home, as the beautiful refrain proclaims:

[4] C.S. Lewis, *Surprised by Joy* (Oxford, England: Bles, 1955), 199.

Come home, come home.
You who are weary, come home.
Earnestly, tenderly, Jesus is calling,
Calling, O sinner, come home!

—WILL L. THOMPSON

Returning to our spiritual home—by moving upward, then inward—unlocks the door to our physical homes. We become the sources of light, salt, and leaven that before were conspicuously absent from our homes. We bring gifts of God with us. Like a child returning home for the holidays, our arms are filled with the presents of God's grace—gifts that flow from the fruit of his Spirit, like love, peace, patience, kindness, goodness, faithfulness, gentleness and self-control (see Galatians 5:23). Upon our lips are the words to the old hymn that we sing as each gift, beautifully wrapped, is opened by its intended loved one:

Amazing grace! (how sweet the sound!)
That sav'd a wretch like me!
I once was lost, but now am found
Was blind, but now I see.
'Twas grace that taught my heart to far,
And grace my fears reliev'd;
How precious did that grace appear
The hour I first believ'd!

Through many dangers, toils, and snares,
I have already come;
'Tis grace that brought me safe thus far,
And grace will lead me home.

—JOHN NEWTON

OUTWARD TOWARD OTHERS

A dearly-departed friend who taught me a great deal about our responsibility to love others has put into a book the following wise and grace-filled words:

At this point I should like to complete the story of my American colleague. He met Jesus Christ; he received Christ as master of his life. Immediately he began to listen to his wife in a quite different spirit. Thus it is with every authentic and living Christian experience. God is passionately interested in each human being. To receive God is also, therefore, to receive his intense interest for those with whom we have rubbed shoulders without really seeing or understanding them. It is impossible to open one's heart to God without also opening it to one's fellow.

The converse is also true, since God is always seeking man so as to set him free from his loneliness and confusion. Every person who sincerely draws close to his neighbor becomes an instrument of divine love, even if one or both of them is unbelieving.

(Speaking of his American colleague again, he writes:)

Basically, however, nothing had changed in his attitude toward his wife. What was needed was an inner illumination, and such illumination is never simply an intellectual matter. It is a spiritual experience.

While he was leading a most thrilling life at the hospital.., back home his wife was dying of emotional starvation. And he had been blind to it all!

This is what the psychiatrist had seen. Psychology thus may reveal problems and suggest wise measures to be taken. But the real solution of problems demands a more profound change, one of a spiritual nature. It is this change in spirit which the Bible calls "metanoia," or "repentance": change of spirit and also self-examination, humiliation, a conscious acceptance of responsibilities hitherto ignored.

... It is quite clear that neither courses nor counseling will ever suffice in the face of our present widespread breakdown of [families]. We need more than good counsel. We need a new moral contagion, one which brings about change in deep-seated attitudes· We need a breath of fresh air, the breath of God's Spirit. No other force in the world can touch a man more deeply in his heart and make him more apt, at last, at understanding others.

Such was the experience of this American couple: a living faith—no longer simply a religion of ideas or sentiment—had transformed their life... to understand each other and to seek together God's leading for [their] home.[5]

I thank God for these words because they reveal the true nature of the Christian message: that once saved we are to be called out of ourselves in the act of listening and responding to the needs of our neighbors. It begins at home, with those kinship ties of love that let the whole world know we are Christians.

God affirms this when He says: "You shall not hate your brother in your heart .... You shall not take vengeance or bear any grudge against the sons of your own people, but you shall love your neighbor as yourself" (Lev. 19:17-18 RSV). Jesus said all the law and the prophets hang on this commandment, and the one commanding us to love God with our entire heart and soul (see Matt. 22:39-40).

Jesus is saying that a person could seek to learn and memorize all the law and prophetic utterances of the Old Testament... or simply live out the spiritual reality of two clear commandments of God! Just think about that for a moment.

In these two commandments, we have the sum of what is truly pleasing to God. We have the very essence of what it means to be "in Christ," to have the "mind of God," and the "power of his Spirit." You see, true Christianity is about

[5] Paul Tournier, *To Understand Each Other* (Richmond, VA: John Knox Press, 1973), 54-57.

relationships! If we move upward in our relationship to God, inward in relationship to self, then outward in relationship to others, we will be harmoniously related to God, self, and each other. The world will see such a harmonious family and find its characteristics of new love, joy, peace, patience, kindness, goodness, faithfulness, meekness, self-control—true contentment infinitely worth possessing. Yes! Others will want what you have!

Our families will become the measure of all that is godly and fair. In them, God will set the standard of truly righteous relationships, where all are in subjection "to one another out of reverence for Christ" (Eph. 5:21).

Then and only then will we consider the needs of the family more important than our own and will seek to live openly, honestly, and actively in love with each member. This will occur not because we have the power to make it happen, but because "greater is he [God] that is in [us], than he [Satan] that is in the world" (1 John 4:4).

What does all this mean to me? It means the same power that raised Jesus from the grave will be available to me and my family. It is not some magical, mythical power promised by the Wizard of Oz, but God's real and lasting power that will protect my home from any monstrous twister seeking to dislodge me from this world and send me sailing somewhere over the rainbow.

Such is the "Rock of Ages" upon which my house is built, where I rest in God's promise that "Every one then who hears these words of mine and does them will be like a wise man who built his house upon the rock; and the rain fell, and the floods came, and the winds blew and beat upon that house, but it did not fall, because it had been founded on the rock" (Matt.7:24-25 RSV).

STAYING HOME

Earlier in this chapter, we talked about Kevin, who had experienced a conversion of his own. Handing over his weary and burdened life to the Lord, he began to embrace "the peace of God, which transcends all understanding" (Phil. 4:7). That leap in the logic which passes human comprehension was just what the doctor ordered. And Kevin would be the first to tell you that although his decision to come home and accept the total, unconditional forgiveness of God was the perfect prescription, staying home and allowing healing to take place was another matter entirely.

In the movie version of *The Wizard of Oz* we really aren't told how long Dorothy continued her convalescence from that nasty bump on the head. But one thing is certain: surrounded by friends and family, she wasn't about to go wandering after her own heart's desire any time soon. And that's as it should be. To stay home and heal will take the help of the best community has to offer—with its emphasis on relational accountability and covenant love.

Because I believe accountability to be so important and

necessary for the family to exist, I have devoted one last chapter to considering the extraordinary strength that comes when two or three are gathered in Christ's name (see Matt. 18:20). In such gatherings we acquire a united energy in helping each other in the endless adventure of discovering, by God's grace, who we really are and who we were always meant to be. Finally, we learn to embrace a contentment that can only come when we live in the company of God and each other.

Twelve

Community & Accountability: Showing Others the Way Back Home

It took a lion with great courage, a tin man with great heart, and a scarecrow with great brains to help Dorothy remain steady on the course of getting back to Kansas. Perhaps it was the combined efforts of this odd foursome that meant the eventual demise of the Wicked Witch of the West. What Dorothy could never have accomplished by herself proved an easier task with three friends walking beside her. Neither the Scarecrow, Tin Man, or Lion, likewise, would have had their needs fulfilled if Dorothy hadn't come along. It's as if they were all drawn together by some common inadequacy.

Yes, "misery loves company!" But it's much more than that, isn't it? The simple truth is that "no man is an island."

Dorothy could no more go it alone than any of us. Like most of human experience, few things in life are ever accomplished without the help of much-needed family and friends. Obviously Dorothy knew this to be true at some deep, subconscious level. In her incredible fantasy, the Scarecrow, Tin Man, and Lion were really farm hands Hunk, Zeke, and Hickory—no doubt, sent by her psyche to aid her in her hour of need. Even in the fantasyland of Oz, it would be those of her own household who would eventually show Dorothy the way back home!

So it is with you and me. We can't make it alone. A vital part of the Christian message is that we're not meant to. We *need each other*! In community, joys are doubled and fears are cut in half. Wisdom is increased and strength is multiplied. My hands become your hands, so our labor is shared. My legs become your legs, so we do not walk alone. This is community in which God says, "Two are better than one ....If one falls down, his friend can help him up.... If two lie down together, they will keep warm.... Though one be overpowered, two can defend themselves" (Ecc. 4:9-12). The conclusion of the matter is that "A cord of three strands is not quickly broken!"

In Chuck Colson's best-selling book, *The Body*, he details the indispensable role of community when he writes that the word for fellowship "describes a new community in which individuals willingly covenant to share in common, to be in submission to each other, to support one another and 'bear one another's burdens,' as Paul wrote to the Galatians, and to build each other up in relationship with the Lord."[1] But Colson doesn't end there, he goes on to talk about how such a new community demands accountability:

Fellowship is more than unconditional love that wraps its arms around someone who is hurting. It is also tough love that holds one fast to the truth and the pursuit of righteousness. For most Christians, the support side of the equation comes more easily than accountability and the subsequent discipline involved. Which is one reason the behavior of Christians is often little different from the behavior of non-Christians. Maybe it's because we simply haven't taught accountability. Or maybe it's because, in today's fiercely individualistic culture, people resent being told what to do, and since we don't want to "scare them off," we succumb to cultural pressures.

Even pastors at times seem reluctant to demand accountability. As in the case of a young couple, unmarried and living

---

[1] Chuck Colson with Ellen S. Vaughn, *The Body* (Dallas: Word Publishing, 1992), 129.

together, who asked a well-known evangelical pastor to marry them. Years earlier the young woman had belonged to the church and sung in the choir. Without further inquiry and without counseling, the pastor agreed to perform the ceremony.

Another equally prominent evangelical had on his payroll a recent convert who was living with his girlfriend. The pastor's counsel? "Think about getting married soon." Extreme examples? I would hope so.

But too often we confuse love with permissiveness. It is not love to fail to dissuade another believer from sin any more than it is love to fail to take a drink away from an alcoholic or matches from a baby. True fellowship out of love for one another demands accountability.[2]

It is to this "true fellowship" we turn next—first, to discuss a masculine perspective of community and then a feminine one. Then we focus on home as the principal laboratory where community and accountability are best taught and where the basis for lasting friendships are first experienced. But we begin with an attempt to explore one of the most universal needs of humankind—the need to be heard! Isn't that what Dorothy wanted when she ran home to family and friends? She instantly blurted out: "Just listen to what Miss Gulch said she was going to do to Toto!"

[2] Ibid., 130.

To be heard is to be unburdened, says Paul Tournier, who sets the stage for our discussion to come:

> We need to see that universal sickness, that innumerable throng of men and women laden down with their secrets, laden down with their fears, their sufferings, their sorrows, their disappointments, and their guilt. We need to understand how tragically alone they find themselves. They may take part in social life, may even play a leading role there, chairing club meetings, winning sports championships .... Yet what eats away at them from within is that they may live years without finding anyone in whom they have enough confidence to unburden themselves.[3]

THE MASCULINE COMMUNITY:
TURNING HEARTS TOWARD HOME

In an article entitled "Finding New Friends on the Block," Mike Yorkey and Peb Jackson describe the 90s trend of men coming together to talk about their feelings and develop deeper relationships with their own gender. Quoting NFL pass receiver Steve Largent, they write, "Men have very few friends whom they feel they can reveal everything to. A lot of men don't have anybody—not even their wives—whom they feel comfortable to talk with. By developing relationships with other men, they can open up and express themselves

[3] Paul Tournier, *To Understand Each Other* (Richmond, VA: John Knox Press, 1973), 49.

freely. "[4]

A Spring '93 issue of *Image* magazine suggests that men are getting together in such accountability groups for one main reason: To reclaim their families! Families are becoming the focus, then, as a new masculine community is evolving with the biblical challenge to turn the hearts of fathers and husbands toward home (see Mal. 4:6; Luke 1:17). Such a focus may seem unusual in light of previous trends, but according to the University of Colorado's football coach, Bill McCartney—who was able to pack Folsom Stadium with over 50,000 men in the summer of '93—fathers and husbands are being motivated and equipped to keep their word with their wives, children, church, and community.[5]

Who are these men?

According to the nation's experts they are veterinarians, ministers, investors, military personnel, businessmen, police officers, postal workers, and body builders. They represent all races, all socioeconomic backgrounds, and all parts of the country. They come together to heed the prophetic words of Howard Hendricks, a Dallas Theological Seminary professor, who said, "A man who is not in a group with other men is an accident waiting to happen."

In the book *Heart of the Warrior*, published in 1993, co-author Michelle Morris and I tell the story of one man who,

[4] Mike Yorkey and Peb Jackson, "Finding New Friends on the Block," *Focus on the Family* (June 1992), 2.

[5] Bill McCartney as quoted in "The Promise Keepers," *Focus on the Family* (June 1992), 4.

with the help of two other men, was able to accomplish extraordinary things by meeting once a week for prayer and accountability. I include a significant portion of his experience here because I believe it bears repeating:

A father with a young son was in prayer one day and felt compelled to go to another man to ask him to pray with him. He felt powerless to achieve his dreams and goals without the other man's help. As the dad began to share his weaknesses, an immediate bond formed between the men. His confessions were superficial at first, but convicted by the Spirit, he began to allow himself to become vulnerable. The friend knew of another man who should join them for their weekly prayer time, so the two quickly became three.

They met every Tuesday without fail, to be an encouragement in prayer to one another, to lift up their burdens, and to claim the blessing that comes when two or three gather together in Christ's name. But as the original father said, God had in mind a whole lot more.

"Although some things did change in our lives as we prayed, many did not," he confided. "It quickly became apparent that we would have to confess our sins to God—but in the company of each other. It seemed that somehow, unconfessed sin, sin that was repressed and denied, had power to blackmail us, to keep us in the darkness with a secret life that was hidden from the world. In a great many ways, we were pretending to be something we weren't."

The young dad said that even in private prayer, the men sometimes talked about their sins with God, but never truly confessed them—never laid them at God's feet. They would discuss worry or guilt about their general sinfulness, but they had difficulty admitting that they committed specific sins and naming them. They all soon learned that God doesn't forgive the bad feelings that sin produces; he forgives sin.

"So we had to do the harder work of confessing sin for what it was," the young prayer partner said. "In the company of Christian friends, one brother's prayer of confession became what every other man needed. It broke the ice. When one brother confessed sin, the other two would hold him if he wept and encourage him when he needed it. This was strange stuff for us! But this unusual show of concern ushered in the blessing of God's forgiveness and offered hope to the two men who had yet to open up. As our confessional times became more open and trusting, we discovered we could confess sins, weep openly, and still be accepted as masculine in the company of men we knew and trusted."

As each brother confessed problems and sins in his life, he was drawn closer into the community of prayer warriors—strong, powerful men who had never before wept, who had never before felt the love of deep friendship and true camaraderie with other men. They weren't on a playing field. They were not at war. Yet, they discovered, it was okay, it was masculine, to talk and show genuine concern—even to hug and weep before the Lord.

"We felt a bond," the father said: "We moved from being impersonal, detached individuals to spiritual warriors. We each attacked the sins of our youth—everything from substance addictions and abuse of pornography to violent tempers and angry talk that hurt our wives and children. It was as though we actually engaged in battle against the old enemies of our fathers—those sinful habits that had been passed on to us through negative role modeling and that we in turn would pass on to our children if we did not overcome them."

When King David was dying he called his son Solomon to him and told him to kill off his old enemies—enemies David should have killed, but failed to as he weakened in his old age. David's tolerance of such enemies was leading to horrible sins among his men as they began to betray and murder one another.

In the same way, the modern-day prayer brothers discovered that they often kept sins—those old enemies—in their lives, knowing full well that God wanted them to fight their way free of them.

"When those old enemies had been passed on to us, we hid them in the darkest parts of our worlds," the father recalled. "And so, our enemies continued to hold us in bondage; and, as they did to our fathers before us, keep us spiritually weak." The young men felt they had a form of godliness, but those old enemies hidden in their lives kept them from truly living out their Christianity.

In their prayers, the small group of men began to ask God to help them beat specific sins. With his strength, they began to crush them, one by one—low self-esteem, insufferable feelings of unworthiness, insecurity, sexual sin, chemical addiction and the like.

The young dad described the great feeling of relief he experienced when he and his two friends prayed together: "It was as if two older brothers were assembled with me, picking out my old enemies on the playground of life. As I stood in the protection of these strong brothers, I could watch as those intergenerational bullies fled in terror. We all felt deliverance like none we had ever known—and our lives began to change. It was remarkable."

As the men continued to meet, they left no stone unturned. They continued to delve into every nook and cranny of their lives, searching for sin like warriors with bright spotlights searching for all the hidden remnants in a conquered land.

God's forgiveness covered them with peace—not because of some perfect confessional technique, but because God's grace is greater than any sin. He answered their prayers, and responded to their spirit of repentance.

Sometimes their prayers dealt with their marriages and their inability to properly love their wives.

"The old enemies of our fathers and the sins of our youth had haunted us and kept us from being the husbands we needed to be," one young man said. "And so those sins needed to be drawn and quartered, crushed, pulverized—destroyed like the others so they, too, no longer had any power over us. Once loosed, I felt the freedom to love as I had never loved before—as if a ball and chain were gone and I could glide effortlessly to the wife of my youth and make her needs mine."

Sexual addiction was in their way, the prayer brothers confessed.

"The beauty of our wives was lost amidst the lies of pornographic manipulation," they explained. "It caused us to believe the falsehood that the grass is greener anywhere else but at home. It caused us to believe that our sexuality wasn't being fulfilled, suggesting that we needed something more than our wives could provide. Now, with the enemy gone, our wives looked lovelier to us than ever. We were touched once again by those things that drew us to them in the beginning.

"With the enemy in full retreat, we could again see our wives as Jesus sees them: brides without spot or blemish. Again we saw their moral loveliness, and we found them infinitely worth embracing. With the enemy gone, we could remember what we had forgotten: 'They are the daughters of our King. They are princesses, royalty, bought with a price and sanctified with the blood of our Lord.' We fell in love with them all over again."

The dad also recalled his lack of involvement with his son. He said it was as if he had been blind, deaf, mute and crippled—the very congenital diseases that Jesus chose to heal first—anomalies passed on from former generations. From father to son.

"I was blind because I couldn't see my son's needs. I was deaf because I couldn't hear his cries for attention. I was mute—I couldn't speak the words of love he so longed to hear. And I was an invalid as far as his needs were concerned. I wasn't where he needed me to be—whether it was a ball game or his PTA program," the young dad confessed.

But in the company of godly, praying men, the healing power of Jesus was unleashed again and whatever spiritual disease that had hampered the father began to leave. He was able to say, "I love you," for the first time, to listen to his son's heart as well as his words. He was there when his son needed him. And, most of all, he saw his son with new eyes—no longer as a burden, but as a blessing; a treasure from God.[6]

Now, that's coming home from over the rainbow to score a home run with the wife and kids! But the real point is: He *couldn't have done it alone.* To be moved in the direction of God—for vigorous challenge and inward movement toward self, for hard-hitting examination—requires the help of a small band of dedicated friends who will not betray confidences.

Chuck Colson agrees. His plea is for a return to a "righteous" community (remember my concept of righteousness being right relationships with God, self, and others) and a kind of "spiritual mentoring"system that includes a series of questions that men challenge each other with periodically:

1 Have you been with a woman anywhere this past week that might be seen as compromising?

2 Have any of your financial dealings lacked integrity?

3 Have you exposed yourself to any sexually explicit material?

4 Have you spent adequate time in Bible study and prayer?

5 Have you given priority time to your family?

6 Have you fulfilled the mandate of your calling?

7 Have you just lied to me?[7]

[6] Michael A. O'Donnell and Michelle Morris, Heart of the Warrior (Abilene, TX: Abilene Christian University Press, 1993), 21-26.
[7] Colson, 131.

The key is that small group accountability must be voluntary. No one should force you to divulge anything you're not comfortable sharing. You should chose the people you want to meet with, yet try to limit the group to two or three. Don't forget: what is said in the small group, stays in the small group!

I like the concept of spiritual mentors as a necessary part of the masculine community. In a section entitled "Men and Mentors," in his book *The Real Man Inside*, Verne Becker describes how older men need to be in the lives of younger men to challenge and nurture their inner, spiritual selves. He goes on to describe this mentoring dynamic:

Several things distinguish a mentor from other older men. First, a mentor has a certain wisdom that he has gained during his life that the younger man can learn from. In some way he stands out as a role model. Often this comes from working in the same field. Second, he's much more interested in what's going on inside rather than outside of the younger man; in other words, he cares about the man's soul and tries to nourish it. He helps a man to focus on what's really important. Third, the mentor is a "seer" in the sense that he sees things that the man may not be able to see in himself—blind spots and short-comings, but also strengths and gifts. He is able to remain impartial about these traits, however, because he doesn't carry the emotional baggage of the man's father. He can simply call attention to them to help the man grow. Sometimes he advises, sometimes he challenges, sometimes he criticizes; but it is clear that he does it out of concern for the man's inner development. Fourth, and closely related to the third, a mentor gives the man a sense of being recognized and a hint of where his destiny may lie. He calls forth greatness from the man.[8]

In our search for a mentor, Becker suggests that we need to think "of men we admire, men who could serve as a role model." Much of what he describes reminds me of the apostle Paul's relationship with his young apprentice Timothy. It shows how a man can be empowered by the love and acceptance of an "adopted" spiritual father, in addition to his earthly one.

For those of you who don't know, Timothy was a man of God who received his faith and knowledge of God through his maternal lineage: his grandmother Lois and his mother Eunice (see 2 Tim. 1:5). In fact, the book of Acts explains that Timothy's father was a Greek, not a Hebrew, and therefore was probably not equipped in any spiritual way to teach Timothy what he would need to know about manhood in a Jewish community.

Because Timothy received the faith from the women in his life, the authors of Heart of the Warrior speculate that he probably never had a chance to observe his father acting as the spiritual leader for his family or as the conduit for the word of God to be spoken into Timothy's life. Therefore, in

[8] Verne Becker, The Real Man Inside (Grand Rapids, MI: Zondervan Publishing House, 1992), 120-121.

his role of spiritual leadership and responsibility, Timothy had what the Bible identifies as a "spirit of timidity" (2 Tim. 1:7). Although this "spirit of timidity" is not clearly understood, the apostle Paul may be trying to shed some light on the subject by intimating that perhaps Timothy was struggling with a lack of a male role model in his life and the great insecurity it produced. Therefore, Paul "adopted" Timothy as his son, becoming his spiritual father and mentor.

Paul reminds him to "fan into flame the gift of God," which was in Timothy through the laying on of Paul's hands (2 Tim. 1:6). In so doing, Paul provided Timothy with a blessing passed from father to son—something Timothy perhaps did not receive from his own earthly dad.

Why was that blessing so important? So that Timothy, who was a gifted leader of the early church, would not have to go before the masculine community of his day feeling as though something was lacking in his life... or that somehow he was not manly enough... or even that he was not old enough to be called to such an important role within Christendom.

Paul's instructions to Timothy often sound like a father's instructions to his son to enable him, to empower him, and to pass on the mantle of manhood. This becomes more obvious in 2 Tim. 2:22, when Paul tells Timothy: "Flee the evil desires of youth, and pursue righteousness, faith, love and peace, along with those who call on the Lord out of a pure heart." In 1 Cor. 13: 11, Paul uses somewhat parallel language about young faith versus mature faith: "When I was a child, I talked like a child, I thought like a child, I reasoned like a child. When I became a man, I put childish ways behind me."

By adopting Timothy as his spiritual son, Paul is calling for him to become a man, to become a viable member of the masculine community!

Becker warns, however, that when building a relationship with a mentor, we should not make him into a literal father-figure. "Fathers are too likely to step in and control their sons," he writes. "They can't be objective. A mentor, on the other hand, didn't change your diapers.... He can call the shots as he sees them.... While a mentor can help a younger man resolve some of his father issues [as is the case, I believe, with my example of Paul and Timothy], he cannot and should not try to step into the father's role."[9]

It's interesting that Robert Schuller, in his book *Power Ideas for a Happy Family*, agrees that the family is the original small accountability group. In asking the question, "What is a family?" he describes a place where a few people form a caring, sharing, bearing, baring, daring, small therapeutic fellowship.[10] He continues: "In this small group the members are blunt, at times almost cruel with each other.... What other kind of social structure is there where you can tell people right to their faces what you think and know, in a loving relationship for the purpose of helping each other?"[11]

[9] Ibid., 122.

[10] Robert Schuller, *Power Ideas for a Happy Family* (Old Tappan, NJ: Fleming H. Revell Company, 1972), 19.

[11] Ibid.

Schuller makes a wonderful point that much of contemporary mental illness is the result of people who have never learned to take criticism and accept discipline, because they grew up in families where there was a total lack of accountability. "When they get into the brutal, hard-hitting, tough world, they can't take it," Schuller concludes. "When faced with a problem—[they] run!"[12]

And for many Americans, running away means searching somewhere over the rainbow for what only our families were meant to provide.

Obviously, the whole point of this book is to get us to return home, to get us to think about what's right with our families versus what's wrong with them. It's a fundamental belief that it's never too late to change, that families can adapt, that when all is said and done, the family is the one place where you can be accepted and loved "even when they have seen and heard you at your worst."[13] When no one else cares, they do. When everyone shuts you out, they let you in. If forming same-sex friendships ultimately shows us the way home, then great! If they merely become a substitute for our families, then I believe they have gone too far and have overstepped the boundaries where small group accountability ends and the sacred rights and the blessed privileges of the family begin.

[12] Ibid.
[13] Ibid.

THE FEMININE COMMUNITY; GIFTED FOR INTIMACY

Because men value what psychology calls a "territorial imperative"—like the invisible geographical boundary dogs create with their scent—they have often found intimacy with other men difficult to achieve. Thus, like dogs, their body language often says, in not-so-subtle ways, "if you get too close I'll either run or bite." On the other hand, women seem less concerned with boundary maintenance. They have an extraordinary giftedness for intimacy.

Dee Brestin agrees in her book, *The Friendships of Women*. She takes a close look at the power of the feminine community and its pattern for friendship that can unleash and channel a woman's gift for intimacy. This gift, she says, may stem from the fact "that since the mother is almost always the primary care giver in childhood, girls have experienced a deep same-sex friendship in their formative years, whereas boys have not."[14]

This is a powerful observation because it assumes that the converse could also be true. That is, if fathers would assume a more active role in parenting, then perhaps men's friendships would become increasingly more acceptable! I couldn't agree more.

Another powerful observation by Brestin is that the feminine community sees itself in a web of relationships. "My husband and I have noticed," she writes, "that when we ask

[14] Dee Brestin, *The Friendship of Women* (Wheaton, IL: Victor Books, 1988), 24.

members of a Sunday school class to introduce themselves with a thumbnail sketch, the women will invariably mention their relationships with others, whereas men will simply talk about themselves."[15] This very real difference, I believe, gives us a focus for the feminine community that will be largely different than that of the male's.

Whereas the principal focus of the masculine community needs to be on the development of familial relationships in the home—especially as father, husband, and brother—the feminine community, by contrast, needs to be focused on the empowering of itself to value women as much as men. This third observation by Brestin, although almost hidden in her text, is really one of the most profound. "God may choose to meet our needs through women," she concludes, "but if we value them less than men, we may not see it."[16]

Thus, if men need mentors as necessary role models in the areas of fathering and husbandry, then in other ways it is true that women need mentors to remind them of their immense value as human beings regardless of whether they are career women, wives, mothers, or all three! They need to know their gift of intimacy will no doubt bless their families and friends with immeasurable joy; and like Dorothy Gail from Kansas, bring in all those scarecrows, tin men, and cowardly lions to accomplish together what they would have been powerless to accomplish alone.

[15] Ibid., 36.
[16] Ibid., 63.

Who can forget the tender, parting words of the Tin Man to Dorothy before she heads back home? "I know I have a heart, because it's breaking."

Dorothy had taught him love, with all of its potential for happiness as well as heartache—something she had learned from her family back in Kansas.

She had also given the three friends the gift of each other. They could finally survive without her because they had become community, one in which they would continue to harness the power of heartwarming, heartrending relationships!

THE FAMILY AS COMMUNITY:
IN DEFENSE OF THE GREATEST INSTITUTION ON EARTH

"What happens in your house," says Barbara Bush, former First Lady of the United States, "makes more difference than what happens in the White House." I agree! "For as the family goes, so goes the nation." I'm not sure who said that first, but social scientists are finally beginning to acknowledge the strategic positioning of families to promote the well-being of whole societies.

There is great truth to the statement that our families are a symbolic mirror in which we see reflected the problems of an entire nation. In the long run, I believe the values and behaviors of America's families will ultimately determine our national strength. To strengthen the family is to strengthen the nation.

Dr. Armand M. Nicholi, a faculty member at Harvard Medical School, draws an important parallel between the emotional health of the family and the stability of future generations. "Early family experience," he writes, "determines our adult character structure, the inner picture we harbor of ourselves, how we see others and feel about them, our concept of right and wrong, our capacity to establish the close, warm, sustained relationships necessary to have a family of our own, our attitude toward authority and toward the Ultimate Authority [God] in our lives, and the way we attempt to make sense of our lives."[17]

Certain trends, concludes Nicholi, could "incapacitate the family, destroying its integrity, and cause its members to suffer such crippling emotional conflicts that they will become an intolerable burden to society." Make no mistake about it: families are a necessary and indispensable part of character development and emotional stability. By returning to them we acknowledge the things they can provide us that cannot be attained outside of the family realm.

The family's provision of satisfaction, love, fulfillment, and security—coupled with a sense of belonging—are exactly the things Dorothy longed for and ultimately came to understand couldn't be found over the rainbow.

Add to that list *values*. Dorothy discovered that Oz lacked some fundamental values that she had learned from

[17] Armand M. Nicholi, "The Fractured Family: Following It Into the Future," *Christianity Today* (25 May 1979), 9-15.

childhood. "I keep forgetting," she would say, "I'm not in Kansas anymore." Remember? Witches that terrorized communities of "little people"; lions that preyed on weak, defenseless dogs; and trees that scolded humans for eating fruit from their limbs all reminded Dorothy that she wasn't at home, where life was fairly predictable.

Dorothy brought values to Oz—values that placed a premium on human relationships, values that greatly conflicted with an evil monarchy and a less-than-benevolent Wizard of Oz. While the Wicked Witch of the West placed a value on personal power, Dorothy was more than willing to surrender her ruby slippers for friends and family back home. It was not even Dorothy's original intention to kill the Wicked Witch. She was simply trying to save a friend from burning to death when she struck that fatal blow.

As she melted before their eyes, the Wicked Witch exclaimed: "What a world! What a world! Who would have thought that a good little girl like you could destroy my beautiful wickedness?!"

The Witch thought she was invincible. Untouchable. She thought that in her world of "might over right" she reigned supreme. Yes, indeed! Who would have thought that a good little girl like Dorothy could put an end to her malevolent empire? But she did.

Truly evil people always have a tendency to underestimate the power of good. Although the Wicked Witch acknowledged Dorothy's moral goodness, she believed it to be to her ultimate advantage and Dorothy's eventual demise. How wrong she was. Even in our nation, I believe the right values can overcome discrimination, poverty, even racism, if good little boys and girls are taught to value the fundamental rights of all people, beginning in their own homes.

It is interesting to note that Dorothy brought hope to an otherwise dark and dismal palace, where guards, like robots, served the Witch's every whim. "Hail to Dorothy, the Wicked Witch is dead!" became their liberating cry. Even in the Emerald City, she brought the Wizard out of hiding to openly and honestly face the truth and function within a community he had shunned for years. She had brought values from home that changed Oz forever. In her last dying moments, the Wicked Witch would acknowledge that change with the words: "What a world! What a world!" Yes, indeed, her world was gone—transformed by the most unpredictable of social activists, a simple, decent child who valued love over power, servanthood over greed, and friendship over betrayal.

Bruce C. Birch, in his book *Let Justice Roll Down*, would not be surprised by Dorothy's social witness and might explain that such was the expectation placed upon Israelite families when in similar circumstances. In his chapter entitled "The Old Testament Story as Moral Resource," he says it is the task of a religious community in a strange land—and, no doubt Dorothy thought Oz was a strange land—to foster a loving response to otherwise challenging circumstances. He continues:

The task in exile, according to Jeremiah, is to build community there, in the midst of Babylon. They are to build houses, plant gardens, conduct marriages, and have children (vs. 5-6). But Jeremiah's advice takes an even more surprising turn. "But seek the welfare of the city where I have sent you into exile, and pray to the Lord on its behalf, for in its welfare you will find your welfare." (Jer. 29:7) In the place of the vengeance many would desire (see Ps. 137:8-9) the prophet sets the task not only of becoming community in the midst of the empire but of learning to live there for the sake of the welfare (shalom) of the empire. The prophet suggests a vocation of creative minority in the larger social realities of the world that remains pertinent through the remainder of the biblical period (Old Testament and New), for seldom after the period of exile was the Jewish community or the early church able to live a political existence apart from the reality of a larger political empire. Such a model is, of course, suggestive for modern Christian life in the midst of larger sociocultural realities. The role of intentional creative minority is an option open to those who feel that the church is endangered by more accomodationist models of community; but Jeremiah's words stand as a warning that such community in the midst of empire (majority culture) must be for the sake of that majority culture.[18]

This clear teaching of God, concludes Birch, gives potential guidelines for a community capable of maintaining

[18] Bruce Birch, *Let Justice Roll Down* (Louisville, KY: John Knox Press, 1990), 304.

identity and conjugal and kinship ties in the face of disinte-
grating cultural pressures.[19] Coming home from Oz to view
the role of family as a sacred group capable of bringing
contentment to our restless hearts may well save an empire,
and so establish peace on earth and good will toward men.

[19] Ibid., 305.